Mission, Meaning, and Money:

How the Joint Distribution Committee Became a Fundraising Innovator

MARK I. ROSEN

Afterword by Jonathan D. Sarna

Fisher-Bernstein Institute for
Jewish Philanthropy and Leadership
Brandeis University

iUniverse, Inc.
New York   Bloomington

iUniverse books may be ordered through booksellers or by contacting:

iUniverse
1663 Liberty Drive
Bloomington, IN 47403
www.iuniverse.com
1-800-Authors (1-800-288-4677)

Because of the dynamic nature of the Internet, any Web addresses or links contained in this
book may have changed since publication and may no longer be valid. The views expressed
in this work are solely those of the author and do not necessarily reflect the views of the
publisher, and the publisher hereby disclaims any responsibility for them.

ISBN: 978-1-4401-6741-6 (sc)
ISBN: 978-1-4401-6742-3 (ebook)
ISBN: 978-1-4401-6743-0 (dj)

Printed in the United States of America

iUniverse rev. date: 01/27/2010

This book is dedicated to my father, Samuel Rosen, who supported Jewish causes throughout his life and who benefitted from support provided by the American Jewish Joint Distribution Committee in post-war Europe.

Table of Contents

ACKNOWLEDGMENTS

In a work about fundraising and philanthropy, it is fitting to begin these acknowledgments by mentioning the generous contributions of those who made this study possible.

Major support for Mission, Meaning, and Money was provided by Stanley Snider of Newton, Massachusetts, and by Leslie Schultz, Jaynie Schultz, and Ron Romaner of Dallas, Texas to honor their husband, father, and father-in-law Howard Schultz for his ongoing dedication to the American Jewish Joint Distribution Committee.

Additional support was provided by William M. Marcus, a member of the JDC board, and by Jonathan G. Davis, Michael G. Frieze, Marjorie Grodner Housen, William R. Sapers, James H. Shane, and Justin L. Wyner.

At Brandeis University, Amy Sales, director of the Fisher-Bernstein Institute for Jewish Philanthropy and Leadership, was responsible for launching and directing this project and provided institutional support and funding. Len Saxe, director of the Cohen Center for Modern Jewish Studies, also provided institutional support and funding. I thank them for creating a research environment that attracted a project of this caliber.

While lengthy writing projects are ultimately solitary endeavors, they cannot be completed without help. I was fortunate to have an outstanding research assistant at Brandeis, MeLena Hessel. Each time I made a request, she responded with an extensively researched and carefully organized document that far exceeded my expectations. She is the smartest and most diligent person who ever worked for me.

I also thank Deborah Grant for her valuable editorial assistance.

Without JDC's gracious cooperation, this study could not

have been written. Steve Schwager, JDC's executive vice-president and chief executive officer, agreed to participate in this project with no stipulations and granted full access to JDC staff and board members for interviews. Eliot Goldstein, JDC's deputy director for Global Resource Development served as the liaison for this project over the course of several years, facilitating contacts and responding to numerous requests. Working with him was always a pleasure. He epitomizes both the professionalism and talent of JDC staff. I am deeply grateful to Alan Gill, JDC's executive director for International Relations, for illuminating the intricacies of fundraising at JDC, for explaining the political dynamics of the federation system, and for offering his wisdom and support during numerous conversations. Jonathan Kolker, who served as president of the JDC board during a key transformative period, provided valuable background information and shared his unpublished manuscript, which proved to be essential reading for understanding recent federation system history.

This book underwent an extensive review process. In addition to receiving feedback from Steve Schwager, Eliot Goldstein, Alan Gill, and Jonathan Kolker at JDC, I also received helpful comments from Ed Bayone, Rebecca Caspi, Judge Ellen Heller, David Mersky, Steve Noble, Asher Ostrin, Amy Sales, Jonathan Sarna, Ted Sasson, Michael Schneider, and Jack Ukeles. I appreciate their time and conscientiousness. This is a better book as a result of their input.

A total of 83 individuals were interviewed for this book. All of them were passionate about helping world Jewry, regardless of their institutional affiliations. I want to express my appreciation for their time and hope that the final product accurately reflects their recollections and observations regarding JDC.

Barry and Merle Ginsburg deserve special thanks for their extraordinary candor and openness. Their story is the basis for Chapter 9 of this book. I hope it inspires others to similar levels of caring and generosity.

Finally, I wish to thank my wife Sarita Ledani Rosen for her love and support.

INTRODUCTION

About the American Jewish Joint Distribution Committee

The American Jewish Joint Distribution Committee, an international Jewish relief organization with an annual budget of over $350 million, provides programs and services primarily to Jewish communities in over 70 countries around the world. According to executive vice-president and chief executive officer Steve Schwager, it is the largest American Jewish charity in terms of annual expenditures.

Known affectionately as "The Joint" by insiders, and referred to more generally by the acronym JDC, the organization is largely unfamiliar to the general public. JDC has a low profile because of the nature of its work and because it does not operate like most other nonprofits.

Historically, JDC has deliberately chosen not to draw attention to itself so as not to compromise its field operations. Sometimes, its activities have been conducted in countries where officials were openly hostile to Jewish citizens, making it necessary for JDC to conduct its activities covertly.

JDC does not raise money in conventional ways. Nor does the organization offer typical volunteer opportunities, since its programs are offered exclusively overseas. For all of these reasons, it remains largely unknown to Americans. Yet, in countries where JDC offers programs and services, it enjoys a high level of recognition.

Founded at the beginning of World War I to aid suffering Jews in Europe and the territory then known as Palestine, the organization's mission has remained constant over the years. JDC rescues Jews when their communities are threatened, provides relief to Jewish communities in distress, and offers renewal programs to Jewish communities that are rediscovering their heritage. It also helps Israel address its most pressing social problems and provides non-sectarian relief in almost 30 countries.

Despite the organization's lack of visibility, its fundraising revenues continue to grow annually. How is it that an organization with such a low level of recognition – an organization that generally does not advertise, engage in direct mail campaigns, or conduct telephone solicitations – raises $120 million in a single year? This book attempts to answer this question. The reader is forewarned, however, that the answer is both deceptively simple and maddeningly complex.

The simple explanation for JDC's fundraising success is that it has a sophisticated fundraising operation that effectively makes the case for the importance of the organization's work. When donors learn about what JDC does, they are moved to support its programs.

The maddening complexity comes into play when one begins to examine the organizational framework within which JDC operates. Ever since the first Jews came to America in 1654, Jewish communities have created organizations to provide assistance to their fellow Jews, in this country and abroad. The American Jewish Joint Distribution Committee is one of these organizations. Simultaneously, JDC is also a recipient of funds raised by other Jewish organizations for the purpose of assisting overseas Jewry. Because JDC's funding sources are so intertwined with other major Jewish organizations, the environment in which it raises money is considerably different from that of a typical nonprofit. JDC's fundraising activities are subject to many unique constraints, making its success all the more remarkable.

From shortly after its founding until just before World War II, JDC did its own fundraising. Then, in 1939, in order to improve its ability to raise money, it co-created a new fundraising entity in conjunction with a sister agency, the United Palestine

Appeal.[1] The new organization, which was called the United Jewish Appeal, enabled both agencies to focus on programs and services rather than funding. For almost 60 years, JDC received its funding from the United Jewish Appeal and did not have to worry about raising money directly.

By the late 1990s, however, this funding arrangement was no longer sufficient. The fall of communism had given JDC first-time access to millions of Jews in Central and Eastern Europe and the former Soviet Union who had been cut off from the West. Despite their new freedoms, many were choosing to remain in their home countries rather than emigrate. As economies in these countries slowly transitioned from communism to capitalism, social services suffered, and Jewish citizens struggled. JDC neither anticipated nor planned for the massive needs that emerged. Helping these Jews was central to JDC's mission. However, the American philanthropic funding system that allocated money to help overseas Jewry was not responsive, and JDC could not obtain anything close to the additional $90 million that it estimated it would need each year.

For the most part, the attention of American Jewry and the vast majority of donations were directed not to those Jews who had chosen to stay in their home countries, but to those who had chosen to leave. Almost a billion dollars were raised from American donors to help those emigrating from the former Soviet Union to Israel or the United States. However, only about $15 million went to support JDC's programs to help Jews who remained.

As far as American Jewish philanthropy was concerned, "out of sight" was "out of mind." JDC had identified significant hunger and poverty among the elderly in thousands of communities and wanted to address these needs, but it

---

[1]   JDC's focus before and during World War II was primarily on European Jewry, while the United Palestine Appeal focused on Palestine, where services to Jews were provided by the Jewish Agency for Palestine. Once the State of Israel was founded in 1948, the two organizations were renamed the United Israel Appeal and the Jewish Agency for Israel, respectively.

could not. JDC lacked the resources to pay for programs, the fundraising framework to make its case directly to donors, and the political influence to change the prevailing ideology, which saw emigration, especially to Israel, as a much higher priority. As a result, JDC started its own fundraising department in 1997. The story would be simple from this point on if JDC had been able to raise money like other nonprofits, but because of the peculiar nature of the organized American Jewish community, it could not. Instead it was constrained by its history and intricate interdependencies with other Jewish organizations.

JDC's funding originated with Jewish federations around the country, each of which sent a portion of its annual campaign revenues to the United Jewish Appeal.[2] Because JDC received its funding from federations, it could not compete with them to raise money, but instead had to work cooperatively. Then, two years after JDC created its fundraising department, the United Jewish Appeal dissolved. A new entity emerged, the United Jewish Communities, changing the entire North American funding system. Now, instead of just receiving a check, JDC had to vie with the Jewish Agency for Israel for a portion of its funding in each federated community. While JDC and the Jewish Agency for Israel had competed for overseas funding since the 1920s, the competition took on a new level of intensity.

The story of how JDC became a quiet fundraising juggernaut in just over a decade is a fascinating one that provides insights into the nature of fundraising and Jewish organizations. But to understand how JDC raises money, and why it is so successful at doing so, one must first understand in some detail the historical and organizational context in which it has operated.

---

2   Much like the United Way, federations are centralized fundraising organizations in Jewish communities that allocate funds to domestic and overseas agencies. Before 1999, overseas allocations were sent to the United Jewish Appeal and then split between JDC and the Jewish Agency for Israel. In 1999, the United Jewish Appeal and the Council of Jewish Federations merged, creating the United Jewish Communities, which is the current coordinating body that serves as an umbrella organization for all 155 federations.

JDC's Business Model and Revenue Sources

JDC's fundraising revenue grew from $8 million in 1993 to $120 million in 2007, and JDC's budget grew from $80 million to $353 million during those same years (see Table A1 in Appendix A for JDC's budget growth). However, yet another pair of figures reveals even more about the organization's transformation over this period. In 1993, 90 percent of JDC's funding was unrestricted. The agency received almost all of its money from the United Jewish Appeal and allocated the funds based on priorities it identified around the world. Fifteen years later, in 2008, only 20 percent of its funding was unrestricted, with only 13 percent coming from the overseas portion of federations' annual campaign revenues collected by the United Jewish Communities. The rest of JDC's budget consisted of designated funding, targeted for specific programs.

JDC has been highly effective at leveraging its unrestricted funding. For every dollar of unrestricted funding it receives, it generates more than four additional dollars in designated funding. JDC works hard to develop relationships with partners – individual donors, Jewish federations, foundations, municipalities and governments – who provide JDC with funding to support specific programs in the countries where it operates.

JDC's single largest funding source is the North American federation system, which provides a total of almost $79 million. Of this figure, $45 million represents unrestricted funding from federations' annual campaign revenues collected by the United Jewish Communities, and the remaining $34 million comes from designated grants provided by individual Jewish federations. Another major source of funds for JDC is Holocaust restitution funding, amounting to approximately $47 million annually in 2006.

While unrestricted funding from the United Jewish Communities and Holocaust restitution funding are major sources of support, neither is included in the $120 million that JDC raises annually through its fundraising operations. This money comes from four sources: designated grants from Jewish federations (as described above), foundations, individual donors, and JDC's board. In 2006, two foundations provided a total of over $21 million to JDC, the Harry and Jeannette Weinberg Foundation of Baltimore, which contributed $13.7 million, and the Chicago-based International Fellowship of Christians and Jews (IFCJ), which donated $7.6 million.[3] JDC's board contributed another $20 million each year.

Where does all of this money go? More than 90 percent of JDC's budget dollars in 2007 were spent providing programs in three geographic areas: Israel (47% of JDC's total budget in 2007); the countries of the former Soviet Union (36%); and Europe (8%).[4] The remainder goes to various countries around the world with much smaller Jewish populations.

JDC is a remarkably efficient nonprofit, with 95 percent of its budget spent on programs and only 5 percent on administration. Fundraising costs are only one cent on the dollar. It is not surprising that Charity Navigator, which rates nonprofits, gives JDC a four-star rating, its highest designation.[5]

JDC's Strengths and Challenges

Nonprofits can be effective at fundraising only if they are well managed. Donors are attracted to and feel more comfortable giving to organizations that are run effectively. JDC has several strengths that contribute to its overall effectiveness and fundraising success:

Professional Staff JDC is a highly decentralized organization in which managers are relatively free to hire their own staff

---

[3] Donation figure for the Weinberg Foundation taken from www. hjweinbergfoundation.org. Donation figure for the IFCJ from www. ifcj.org.

[4] The percentage of the budget spent on Israel in 2007 reflects expenditures of $25 to $30 million to address emergency needs that arose from the country's war in Lebanon in 2006.

[5] See www.charitynavigator.org for more detailed information about JDC's finances.

largely without the involvement of a central human resource function. Throughout its history, JDC has made hiring decisions based not just on specific qualifications but on overall ability and fit with the unique culture of the organization. Michael Schneider, the executive vice-president of JDC from 1988 to 2002, who hired employees based on intuition, and was highly successful at doing so, describes the characteristics of the type of person he saw as a good fit for JDC:

> *A 'Jointnik' is a little bit of a maverick, a generalist, can turn his hand to everything from rescue to conflict resolution to negotiation to speech writing, public speaking, administration, is not afraid to get caught in slightly dangerous situations, turns on a dime, is courageous enough to buck headquarters when necessary, and is just a good overall general manager with a lot of* sechel *[wisdom] and savvy, street smart as well as sophisticated, capable of moving in diplomatic circles, speaking to a cabinet minister or a rough people smuggler from dangerous countries, a wheeler-dealer.[6]*

It is not uncommon for JDC to hire someone and only later figure out what they will be doing. A number of observers have observed informally that JDC has the highest quality professional staff of any major Jewish organization.

Elite Board   The board of the American Jewish Joint Distribution Committee is the envy of the Jewish organizational world. The 150 or so members represent a Jewish Who's Who of wealth, influence, and prestige from the United States, Canada, United Kingdom, Israel, and Australia. Board members are carefully selected by a nominating committee, and expectations for participation and giving are high. Involvement encompasses more than an annual check – board members are strongly encouraged to attend meetings, participate on overseas missions, and contribute time and expertise. Board

---

6   Michael Schneider, interview, February 2, 2007.

members are urged to tell their friends about JDC. New board members are assigned mentors and placed on various area committees to learn about JDC programs in particular regions. Future board leaders are identified early on and rotate through a variety of committee chairmanships to prepare them for major leadership roles.

Professionally-Run Programs Programming, in the words of JDC's previous board president, Judge Ellen Heller, is "the heart of the Joint."[7] JDC addresses such social problems as hunger, poverty, disease, unemployment, illiteracy, homelessness, and social isolation. Programs are targeted at the elderly, children-at-risk, ethnic minorities, immigrants, and disabled individuals. JDC also offers many Jewish renewal programs to educate Jews and provide them with information about their cultural heritage and religion. Program design and implementation is based on state-of-the-art practices. JDC is a highly responsive organization that can mobilize quickly to address the needs of Jews or non-Jews anywhere in the world when unexpected events disrupt their well-being.

Enthusiastic Donors From a fundraising standpoint, JDC programs sell themselves. Former JDC board president Eugene Ribakoff observes: "All you have to do is tell the story. You have to just describe the programs and show people the programs that we are doing. They speak for themselves."[8]

JDC frequently arranges donor visits, known as missions, in the countries it serves. Individuals who experience JDC programs first-hand on these missions invariably return with a deep appreciation for JDC's work and a desire to give. JDC donors' enthusiasm about the work inspires them to share information about the program with others. JDC's donors also have a high opinion of the organization because of its sophisticated, continuous emphasis on donor relations and its policy of allocating 100 percent of all donations directly to programs, relying on its unrestricted funding to cover overhead.

---

[7] Judge Ellen Heller, interview, March 12, 2007.

[8] Eugene Ribakoff, interview, April 27, 2007.

Along with the preceding strengths, JDC faces a number of challenges:

Erosion of Core Funding JDC's unrestricted funding from the federation system has been declining each year, and projections suggest it will continue to decline. Loss of this revenue source forces JDC to seek replacement funding sources. Reductions in core funding decrease JDC's program flexibility, reduce its ability to operate independently, and make it more difficult for JDC to support administrative infrastructure, continue vital programs that may not be inherently appealing to donors, leverage designated funding, and maintain its policy of applying all partner funds directly to programs.

Loss of Holocaust Restitution Funding In 2006, JDC received a total of $47.4 million in Holocaust restitution funds from the Swiss Banks Settlement, the Claims Conference, the International Commission on Holocaust Era Insurance Claims, and several other sources. This money, which helps support the elderly in a number of countries, will eventually disappear as each funding stream expires. If life expectancies of JDC aid recipients exceed funding duration, JDC will be hard-pressed to continue certain vital programs.

Economic Fluctuations JDC raises almost all of its money in the United States but spends it overseas. When the dollar weakens relative to the currency in a particular country, there is a corresponding effect on all JDC programs in that country. A specific percentage reduction in the value of the dollar translates into a corresponding reduction in the program budget.[9] Conversely, when the dollar is strong, JDC is able to do more than anticipated. JDC's budget is thus highly sensitive to currency fluctuations.

Aging Board Eighty percent of JDC's board members are over the age of 60. Since JDC's board is one of its greatest strengths, JDC must capture the interest of a younger generation and

---

[9]   In June 2008, JDC laid off 60 staff members and cut aid to 25,000 program recipients as a result of the weakening dollar. See Jacob Berkman, "JDC Lays Off 60, Says It Will Eliminate Aid Programs," *Jewish Telegraph Agency*, June 17, 2008.

recruit energetic new members who care as deeply about its work as the current generation of board members. JDC has not been particularly successful thus far at doing so.

Tensions in the Former Soviet Union Over the past few years, JDC has received negative media attention regarding several disputes with agencies and leaders in the former Soviet Union, potentially influencing donor perceptions of the organization.[10]

When JDC began to develop programs in the countries of the former Soviet Union, it solicited donors to help build Jewish community centers in order to establish an attractive and dignified physical presence for Jewish life. Previously, under communism, the building of Jewish structures had been forbidden. The centers placed a variety of Jewish programs and organizations under one roof, and when successful, created a synergy that benefited the local Jewish community. In order to cover the operating costs of each building, the model required that local organizations pay rent if they moved to the community center facilities, which some resisted. Furthermore, some organizations took issue with JDC's centralized community center management approach, preferring that the centers be managed by local leaders rather than JDC. As a tactic to influence the outcome of these disputes as well as JDC's American donors, local leaders have, on occasion, turned to the Jewish press to air their grievances when their efforts to influence JDC policies were unsuccessful.

Method

Although this project was undertaken with JDC's full cooperation, it was not funded or commissioned by the organization. The material that follows is a synthesis of interviews, reports, memos, emails, publicity materials, periodicals, books, pamphlets, audio recordings, and other documents about JDC.

---

[10] See, for example, Nathaniel Popper, "Builder of Jewish Life in Russia is Now Accused of Hindering Its Growth," *Forward*, August 24, 2007.

Interviews were the primary source of information. Starting in April 2006, the author interviewed a total of 83 individuals in person and by telephone. Interviewees included: JDC staff, board members, and donors; Jewish federation officials and United Jewish Communities leadership; and Jewish Agency for Israel leadership.

Interviews, which lasted an average of one hour, were recorded and transcribed. Interviews were open-ended and informally structured. Interviewees were asked to describe their own responsibilities and their observations about changes that have taken place in JDC.

The manuscript went through three stages of fact-checking and review. First a select group of individuals consisting of academics and JDC insiders reviewed the first draft. Then all of the interviewees, as well as others mentioned in this case study, reviewed for accuracy those sections of the text in which they appeared. The final version was reviewed for accuracy by senior leadership at JDC.

Interviewees and their primary affiliation during the time period in which their name appears in the case study are listed in Appendix B.

Overview of the Story

The case history is organized into three parts. Part 1: Responding to a World of Need, provides an historical and organizational context for the transformation of JDC. Chapter 1 describes JDC's creation and its responses to the major historical events of the 20th century. Chapter 2 covers JDC's involvement with the former Soviet Union both before and after the fall of communism, and highlights the demands this involvement placed on its budget. Chapter 3 explains the structure of the North American Jewish philanthropic system, describes changing donor trends, and discusses how the funding system and JDC were affected by these trends.

Part 2: JDC Responds to the Changing Environment, describes the new fundraising efforts that JDC initiated so that it could properly respond to the needs of Jews in the former Soviet Union, even while its revenues from the United Jewish Appeal were simultaneously decreasing. Chapter 4 outlines how JDC started a fundraising department, and Chapter 5 relates how its relationships with individual federations and the Jewish federation system as a whole changed as the system itself was transformed. Chapter 6 describes some of the internal changes that took place at JDC when it began to do fundraising.

Part 3: Raising Money, focuses on the specifics of JDC fundraising. Chapter 7 describes in detail how JDC works with individual federations, Chapter 8 discusses the various roles of the JDC board with respect to fundraising, and Chapter 9 provides a detailed description of one donor couple's involvement with JDC.

Intended Readership and Classroom Resources

This case history is the second in a series of examinations of Jewish nonprofits sponsored by the Fisher-Bernstein Institute for Jewish Philanthropy and Leadership at Brandeis University.[11] It is intended for a variety of audiences.

First and foremost, Mission, Meaning, and Money is written for the classroom. Future Jewish leaders in training programs and in undergraduate and graduate classes will find a great deal to examine and discuss regarding the complex world of Jewish organizations.

The case study was also written to provide current Jewish leaders with a comprehensive, behind-the-scenes look at a major Jewish organization and its interrelationships with other organizations. The intent is to provide these leaders with material that will help them reflect upon their own organizations and improve their effectiveness.

In addition, the story contains information about the fundraising process that potentially has value for the nonprofit

---

[11] The first such study of a Jewish nonprofit, *The Remaking of Hillel: A Case Study on Leadership and Organizational Transformation*, is available at http://dcoll.brandeis.edu/handle/10192/22945.

sector in general – for fundraisers, nonprofit leaders, and scholars of nonprofits.

Lastly, those interested in modern Jewish history should find the story informative and revealing. To aid readers who may not be familiar with the Jewish nonprofit sector, every effort has been made to explain unfamiliar terms and provide appropriate background information in footnotes.

Classroom instructors interested in obtaining teaching resources to accompany this book should send an inquiry to fisherbernstein@brandeis.edu.

PART 1: RESPONDING TO A
WORLD OF NEED

Chapter 1: Funding the Work of JDC – An Early History[12]

The Origins of JDC

At the time of the outbreak of World War I in 1914, there were approximately 10 million Jews living in Eastern Europe and 85,000 Jews in Palestine. Conditions for these Jews were already difficult, but once the war began, the level of suffering went from difficult to calamitous as they endured homelessness, persecution, hunger, and disease. Circumstances were especially desperate in Palestine, which at that time was under the control of Turkey. Aligned with Germany, Turkey had cut ties to the West. Palestine's Jews were starving as the result of a blockade and were being attacked regularly.

Although there were a multitude of different Jewish organizations at the time in the United States providing overseas assistance, each Jewish organization focused on its own particular Jewish group, and each operated independently without coordinating its efforts with other rescue and relief organizations. Only an urgent request from the U.S. ambassador to Turkey began to rectify these divisions, resulting in the creation of what would eventually be known as the American Jewish Joint Distribution Committee.

On August 31, 1914, Ambassador Henry Morgenthau, Sr., who was a Jew, sent a Western Union cable to Jacob Schiff, a

---

[12] The material in this chapter is drawn from: Bauer, 1981; Bauer, 1974; Beth Hatefutsoth, 1984; Ginzberg, 1942; Handlin, 1964; Hessel, 2007a; Leavitt, 1953; Raphael, 1982; Sarna, 2004; Schachtman, 2001.

prominent philanthropist who held a leadership role with the American Jewish Committee. The cable read:

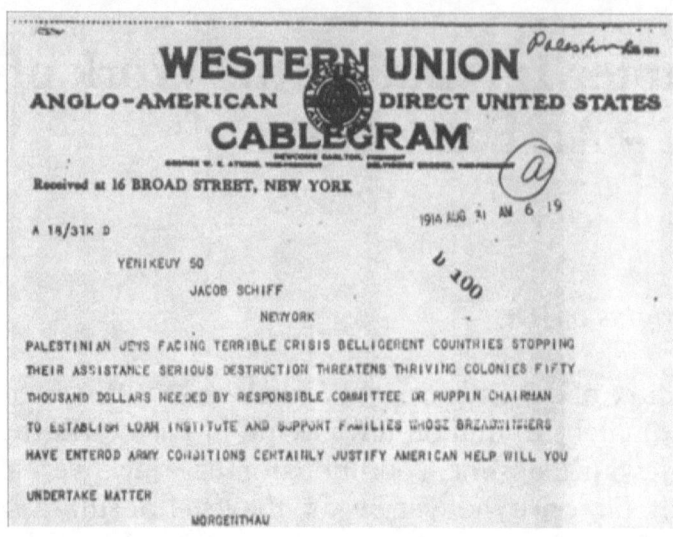

Schiff, with the assistance of the American Jewish Committee, arranged for the funds to be delivered in cash to Palestine. However, even though AJC played a central role in providing aid, the organization recognized its limitations. AJC membership consisted primarily of wealthy German Jews in banking, business, law, and medicine who were affiliated with Reform Judaism. They recognized that they were not representative of American Jews, who had emigrated from a number of different countries and whose religious orientation ranged from Orthodox to atheist. AJC could not address the overseas situation alone. In view of the many relief organizations that existed and the scope of the problems created by the war, AJC saw that only a cooperative framework for relief could address the enormous needs of the time and represent and reach all of the different types of Jews overseas who needed assistance.

Accordingly, on October 25, 1914, AJC convened a group of representatives from 40 national Jewish organizations, resulting in the formation of the American Jewish Relief Committee to raise funds for overseas Jews. However, despite

4

the broad representation, the newly-formed Relief Committee still did not include every Jewish group. Shortly before the AJC meeting, a group of Orthodox Jews with Eastern European origins founded their own organization to address the situation created by the war, which they called the Central Committee for the Relief of Jews Suffering Through the War. The Orthodox group chose not to join the Relief Committee.

The Relief Committee and the Central Committee needed a way to disburse the funds they raised to those in need, so on November 27, 1914, yet another organization was created, the Joint Distribution Committee of American Funds for the Relief of Jewish War Sufferers. The first chair of the Joint Distribution Committee (JDC) was Felix Warburg, Jacob Schiff's son-in-law.

In 1915, the Relief Committee and the Central Committee were joined by a new fundraising organization formed by socialist labor groups, the People's Relief Committee. Each of these groups worked diligently to obtain donations from their respective Jewish constituencies, introducing the idea of mass philanthropy to American Jewry. Almost every Jew gave something. By the end of the war, the three organizations had managed to raise over $16 million ($324 million in present-day dollars) which was then distributed by the Joint Distribution Committee.

Initially, the role of JDC was simply to disburse money to existing relief agencies. However, once the United States entered the war in 1917, JDC had to contend with the political complexities of getting money into countries controlled by Germany, since Germany and the United States were now enemies. JDC's role expanded, and it developed creative strategies to get around the restrictions it faced.

Since JDC, which at this point was comprised entirely of volunteers, was not burdened by fundraising responsibilities, it was able to focus on determining where in Europe and Palestine the money was most needed. Jewish needs were overwhelming. Polish Jews were beset by starvation, homelessness, and pogroms. There were epidemics in the Ukraine, and several hundred thousand Jewish children were now orphans. The Bolshevik Revolution created dislocation and turmoil for Russian Jews. In Lithuania, a number of Jewish shtetls had been obliterated. Romania and Austria were flooded by Jewish refugees.

Despite the fact that it was a newly-formed ad hoc organization, JDC, working closely with American and European relief agencies, took on the enormous task of caring for Jews in need by creating soup kitchens, hospitals, and orphanages, and sending convoys of food, clothing, and medicine to besieged areas. They also provided nonsectarian relief, particularly in Poland, in order to dampen anti-Semitism.

After the war, the Joint Distribution Committee expanded its mission beyond rescue and relief to include the reconstruction of Jewish communities.[13] JDC helped rebuild schools, synagogues, and other Jewish institutions; created a tracing service to reunite families; offered vocational training; and provided interest-free loans. Following the Russian Revolution, over the course of a number of years, JDC helped hundreds of thousands of Jews to resettle in the Crimea and the Ukraine, where they received training as farmers through a program known as Agro-Joint.[14]

Throughout the war and thereafter, cooperation among the various elements of the American Jewish community improved, although relations were by no means harmonious. While the pressing need of the time was undoubtedly a factor, much of the progress resulted from the ongoing efforts of JDC chairman Felix Warburg, a compassionate humanitarian who worked hard to keep the focus on those who were suffering. Although Warburg's leadership style was not democratic, his personal warmth and candor engendered trust among the various factions with whom he worked.

---

[13] The three JDC pillars of rescue, relief, and reconstruction/renewal have remained throughout the years as the core mission of the organization.

[14] See Dekel-Chen, 2005 for a detailed history of these Jewish agricultural colonies.

From the outset, JDC was intended to be a temporary organization, run by Warburg and a small core group of volunteers, which operated according to certain basic principles:[15]

- JDC was apolitical. It did not take sides in various disputes among Jews or between Jews and non-Jews.
- JDC avoided creating long-term dependency relationships with Jews in need. The goal was to provide initial relief and then help create and/or strengthen local institutions that could provide ongoing assistance.
- JDC supported the right of Jews to remain in the countries of their birth or adoption. Although they promoted the right to emigrate, they did not advocate for it.[16]
- JDC maintained that governments should assume their proper share of responsibility in providing aid to their citizenry.
- JDC's core group of volunteers – and only the core – closely supervised the programs and agencies that were selected for support. This principle was somewhat controversial and led to a perception that JDC was paternalistic and not receptive to oversight by others. However, given the ever-changing war circumstances that JDC faced, the rapid responses that were often necessary, and the divisions that existed between religious and secular Jews, this principle gave JDC a great deal of flexibility in emergency situations because its decisions were not complicated and delayed by the need for consultations and democratic votes.

JDC operated under the assumption that it would be disbanded once the wartime emergency ended. By 1921, emergency operations in Europe came to an end, but despite JDC's successful relief efforts, Jewish suffering had not ended. Circumstances were especially difficult for Jews in Poland, which at the time had the world's largest Jewish community.

---

[15] These five principles, like the core mission, have largely continued into the present day.

[16] Subsequent events in Nazi Germany altered this principle.

Each time one crisis abated, another arose. So instead of dissolving, JDC began hiring professional staff, often seeking individuals with a background in social work. In 1925, JDC hired its first professional administrator and reorganized itself according to the different types of aid it provided. By 1931, JDC was finally established as a formal legal entity, adopting its current name, the American Jewish Joint Distribution Committee.

Competition for Dollars: JDC Versus the Zionists

JDC's major focus in its early years was Europe, although it provided considerable resources to Palestine as well. The major donors and supporters of JDC, many of whom were non-religious German Jews, were proud Americans and while sympathetic to and supportive of Jews in Palestine, were not especially sympathetic to Zionism. They felt that the Zionist dream was a fantasy and that Jews should live everywhere. European Zionists, in contrast, fervently sought to create a Jewish state in Palestine and felt it was the obligation of all Jews to relocate there.

The disparate ideologies sometimes generated intense conflicts between JDC leadership and Zionist leadership. In particular, Chaim Weizmann, a British scientist who would subsequently become the first president of the State of Israel, felt strongly that the money being invested in Agro-Joint and other reconstruction projects in Europe by JDC was being wasted and should be spent on Jews in Palestine.

In 1925, the United Palestine Appeal (UPA), a central fundraising body for Palestine, was created by American Zionists, largely as a way to compete with the highly effective fundraising tactics used to generate resources for JDC. In much the same way that the American Jewish Relief Committee had, in 1914, united various fundraising organizations focused on Europe, the UPA united several disparate fundraising organizations that were raising money for Jews in Palestine, such as Hadassah, Hebrew University, and the Jewish National

Fund. Money collected by the UPA in the United States was then sent to the Jewish Agency for Palestine, which had operated as the de facto government for Jews in Palestine since 1923, and to the World Zionist Organization.

Over the next four years, JDC and UPA competed fiercely for donors and dollars while attempting to negotiate some modicum of cooperation. To change this dynamic, the Jewish Agency for Palestine expanded in 1929 to include American Jews who were not committed Zionists.

Felix Warburg was among the new members of the administrative committee. The hope was that this new arrangement would create greater collaboration. Indeed, a $6 million joint fundraising campaign between JDC and the UPA was undertaken in 1930. The plan was that $3.5 million would go to JDC, and $2.5 million would go to UPA. Unfortunately, it was the time of the Great Depression, and the united campaign failed to raise the desired amount. The two organizations went their separate ways again for the next three years.

With tensions rising in Germany, in 1934, at the urging of the leaders of several Jewish communities, the two organizations once again tried to raise money together under a new name, the United Jewish Appeal. This time, the money was to be split according to a prearranged allocation formula, 55 percent for JDC and 45 percent for the UPA. As had been the case several years earlier, the results were disappointing, with each organization raising less than it had done on its own. Nevertheless, they agreed to try joint fundraising again in 1935. This campaign was also not successful.

Despite the poor results, the collaborative fundraising model was appealing. From the perspective of the two organizations, collaborative fundraising meant that they did not need to have separate fundraising personnel, and the same donors did not have to be visited by several different people. The downside of the arrangement was that individual donors could no longer specify whether their money went to Palestine or Europe. In addition, the formula for the "split" was an ongoing source of tension between the two organizations.[17]

Despite a number of attempts, joint fundraising efforts repeatedly yielded less than the two organizations had been able to raise separately, and the sought-after degree of cooperation between JDC and UPA did not occur. Simultaneously, with the rise of Nazism in Germany, JDC became increasingly focused on the growing threat to Jews in Europe, and Zionists became more intent on establishing a Jewish state in Palestine as a refuge. Most of the American non-Zionists who had joined the Jewish Agency for Palestine ended up dropping out, and the two organizations resumed their separate and competing fundraising efforts. The United Jewish Appeal was dissolved in 1935.

The Rising Threat of Nazi Germany

Most of the funds raised for JDC during the 1930s were used to help Jews escape oppression in Germany, Austria, and Czechoslovakia. JDC provided travel expenses, food, shelter, and medical care and helped emigrants obtain scarce seats on ships and trains. By the end of 1939, JDC had helped more than 100,000 individuals emigrate to more than 40 countries, despite the reluctance of most countries to take in Jewish immigrants.

Initially, JDC did not view Palestine as a priority destination for emigrants because of JDC's apolitical stance and donor orientation toward Zionism. Beginning in 1937, the British placed restrictions on Jewish emigration to Palestine, and JDC's policy of not promoting illegal immigration meant that sponsorship of Palestine as a haven was even more problematic.

Not all Jews were willing or able to leave Germany, and JDC provided aid to those who stayed as well. JDC offered vocational training to those who could no longer practice

---

[17] This tension would prevail throughout the remainder of the 20th century, as each organization continually strove to maximize its share at the expense of the other.

their professions and loans to those in financial distress. It also created a school system for Jewish children who could no longer attend Germany's public schools.

It took a devastating pogrom in 1938 in Nazi Germany to bring the separate fundraising efforts of JDC and the United Palestine Appeal back together again. Kristallnacht, which took place over two evenings in Germany and parts of Austria, resulted in over 1,200 synagogues being ransacked and 250 burned. Approximately 8,000 Jewish businesses were vandalized and looted, and 30,000 Jewish men were forcibly sent to concentration camps. The climate for Jews was ominous.

The Federation System and the United Jewish Appeal

Following Kristallnacht, the Zionists reluctantly acknowledged that not all persecuted Jews could escape to Palestine, and given the serious situation in Europe, JDC became more willing to help those who did want to emigrate to Palestine in spite of the complications. In 1939, JDC and UPA agreed to participate in a joint fundraising effort, the United Jewish Appeal for Refugee and Overseas Needs.[18]

The federation system was the driving force behind the creation of this revived version of the United Jewish Appeal. In 1939, 225 American Jewish communities either had a formalized federation or a centralized fundraising campaign, depending upon the size of the community. The federation model had come into existence at the end of the 19th century so that many different Jewish community organizations could receive funds through a single, centralized fundraising function.

The umbrella organization uniting the federations and fundraising groups was the Council of Jewish Federations and Welfare Funds (CJF), established in 1932. It was the CJF that pushed for the creation of the United Jewish Appeal, since it saw the value of a single, national campaign for overseas

---

[18] This new version of the United Jewish Appeal, created by the merger of the fundraising functions of JDC, UPA, and the National Refugee Service, would continue operations for sixty years.

needs with the potential to be more efficient and raise more money. An allocation committee with JDC, UPA, and CJF representation agreed to a fixed amount that each would receive. Any additional money raised would be distributed by the allocations committee.

The 1939 UJA campaign generated over $16 million (almost $237 million in present-day dollars) and was considered a success, since for the first time it raised more than the individual organizations had managed to raise on their own. As a result, the UJA campaign was renewed again for 1940. However, before JDC agreed to participate in the new campaign, it insisted on a change in the allocation formula to a 75/25 split between JDC and UPA, with JDC receiving the larger share. JDC also wanted permission to solicit designated gifts which would go to specific countries.

The negotiations over this allocations formula were acrimonious and lasted for months, with JDC refusing to compromise despite UPA's argument that it would receive less money in 1940 than it had in 1939. The Zionists were furious.

The organizations put on a positive public face for the 1940 campaign, but strong discord existed behind the scenes. By the time of the 1941 campaign, UPA decided to seek funds on its own, setting a goal that was four times the amount it received from the 1940 campaign. JDC followed with its own campaigns and goals. The Council of Jewish Federations was unsuccessful in its efforts to intervene.

Ultimately, given the rapidly deteriorating situation in Europe and overriding need to help suffering Jews, the Council of Jewish Federations was able to bring JDC and UPA back to the negotiating table. In the end, the Zionists received more money than they had in 1940, and JDC received less.

World War II and Its Aftermath

Up until the United States entered the war, JDC was still functioning in countries occupied by Germany. JDC provided shelters and soup kitchens and supported hospitals, child-care centers, and educational programs. In Poland alone, in 1941, over 600,000 Jews were receiving some type of assistance from JDC. Once the United States entered the war, however, JDC could no longer operate openly in countries controlled by the Axis Powers.

In order to help Jews in distress, JDC would therefore have to provide aid covertly. However, there were disagreements between the American and European JDC staff over the extent to which JDC should operate illegally. The American office tended to be more conservative, concerned about JDC's standing. The European office, which was dealing directly with the stark and alarming realities of the war, was more inclined to do whatever was necessary to save Jews and worried less about legal niceties. In order to operate with fewer constraints, JDC relocated its offices from Paris, where the Vichy regime was a danger, to unoccupied Lisbon.

Perhaps JDC's most famous covert operation was its support to the Warsaw ghetto. JDC also supplied money to Swedish diplomat Raoul Wallenberg to help him in his efforts to rescue 15,000 Hungarian Jews. In addition, JDC leased ships, smuggled money to Jewish groups throughout Europe and Asia and sent relief packages to concentration camps.

The United Jewish Appeal raised more than $124 million between 1939 and 1945 ($1.4 billion in present-day dollars), with JDC receiving slightly over half of the total amount. However, relations between JDC and the United Palestine Appeal were still problematic. In 1945, UPA asked for a significant increase in its allocation and opposed JDC's desire to solicit designated gifts for specific countries. After several months of difficult negotiations, UPA conceded the designated gift issue in order to obtain a larger percentage of the split. UPA ended up receiving 43 percent of the money raised, an increase over the original allocation.

After the war, the 1946 UJA campaign, with its slogan "Additional Dollars for the Saving of Additional Lives," turned out to be the most successful to date, generating $102 million (just over $1 billion in present-day dollars) through an unprecedented effort. JDC at this stage was occupied with the enormous post-war tasks of providing medical assistance, setting up Displaced Persons (DP) camps for 250,000 Jews, and feeding those Jews who had returned to their homes. JDC also set up a tracing service, began the process of rebuilding Jewish communities, and helped survivors emigrate to countries around the globe.

JDC had now come around to supporting illegal immigration to Palestine, a process known as *bericha*. As one illustration, the famous ship Exodus, which brought 4,500 Jews from DP camps to Palestine, was purchased in part with JDC money. When it was turned away by the British and the passengers were deported to France, JDC provided them with food, medicine, and clothing.

As more and more Jews sought to emigrate from the ruins of Europe and escape post-war persecution, JDC's expenses mushroomed, and in 1947 it was forced to borrow from New York banks. UPA as well had been borrowing to meet its needs in Palestine. The United Jewish Appeal needed to raise even more money to address the situation.

The Founding of Israel

In the fall of 1947, Zionist leader Chaim Weizmann commenced a fundraising tour of the United States with a new message that portrayed Palestine not as a haven for refugees but as an emerging country needing massive support. He sought to distinguish JDC, which was portrayed as a foreign relief agency focused on Europe, and the UPA, which was building a new Jewish future and a new Jewish nation.

The ideological distinction between aid to Europe and aid to Palestine once again generated a battle over allocations between JDC and UPA for the money raised in the 1948 United Jewish Appeal campaign. But this time, priorities had shifted. The territory previously known as Palestine would become the modern State of Israel, and Israel became the new focus of Jewish concern and fundraising. Israel was a natural destination for Jews in DP camps, and 136,000 of them moved there. Europe now represented the past.

Goldie Myerson, who would later take the name Golda Meir and become Israel's prime minister, was working for the Jewish Agency in Jerusalem at the time. She toured the United States to raise money and generated record-shattering numbers. UPA, at the expense of JDC, received a greater percentage of the money raised than ever before.

Despite these fundraising successes by the Zionists, the leadership of the United Jewish Appeal recognized that fundraising for Israel would be even more effective if it were done by local federation leaders. Most American Jews, although somewhat sympathetic to Zionist ideals, were not active in Zionist causes, and were more likely to give to Israel if approached by someone from their own community. This strategy further strengthened Israel's pre-eminence on the national fundraising agenda as local Jewish leaders joined the cause. JDC, acknowledging that Israel was now the priority, willingly took a back seat to the renamed United Israel Appeal with respect to allocations. By the early 1950s the split had stabilized at roughly 25/75, with UIA receiving the majority.

The massive post-war influx of Jews from Europe's DP camps and elsewhere placed considerable burdens on the new State of Israel. Many of these individuals were ill or disabled. The newly established Israeli government asked JDC and JAFI for help, and the two organizations jointly founded MALBEN, an organization that began to create hospitals, rehabilitation centers, and tuberculosis sanitariums.[19] In 1951, JDC took full responsibility for MALBEN, and the Jewish Agency became responsible for organizing immigration to Israel and for helping to settle new immigrants. MALBEN's role eventually expanded beyond immigrants to include aged, disabled, at-risk, or vulnerable Israelis, and at one point almost half of JDC's worldwide budget went to MALBEN.

In 1975, responsibility for MALBEN institutions was transferred from JDC to the Israeli government, and that same year, JDC created the JDC-Brookdale Institute to conduct

---

[19] MALBEN is a Hebrew acronym for the Organization for the Care of Handicapped Immigrants.

research on social programs. In 1976, JDC took on a new organizational structure that has continued into the present day, creating JDC-Israel to help develop social service and capacity-building programs through partnerships with the Israeli government and other non-profit agencies.

Periodically, after World War II, JDC found itself encountering situations that required it to operate in a clandestine fashion. Such realities as dictatorial regimes, anti-Semitic officials, anti-Israel sentiments, and regional wars placed Jews in danger, requiring JDC to provide aid or evacuate them to safe havens. Jews were secretly evacuated by JDC from the Soviet Union, Yemen, Iran, Iraq, Yugoslavia, Ethiopia, and elsewhere.

These activities imbued JDC with a "cloak and dagger" mystique that served it well. Donors to the United Jewish Appeal did not always know the details of what JDC was doing, but they knew that its activities were extremely important and aided in saving Jewish lives.

The undercover nature of some of JDC's work was unfortunately highlighted in 1967, when Charles Jordan, JDC's executive vice-president, died under mysterious circumstances in Prague, putting JDC onto the front pages. The murder was never solved.

The fundraising activities of the United Jewish Appeal adequately met JDC's needs for nearly four decades. However, starting in the late 1980s, the financial arrangement slowly began to unravel as JDC started to encounter huge, unexpected expenses as a result of new freedoms for Jews in the Soviet Union.

Chapter 2: Upheaval in the Soviet Union

Soviet Emigration[20]

In the late 1960s, the Soviet Union began to allow a trickle of Jews to emigrate to Israel if they had family members there, and if they did not possess information deemed vital to Soviet national security. Emigration by Jews to other countries was not allowed. Since there were no direct flights between the Soviet Union and Israel, those who received approval by the Soviet government first traveled to Vienna, where they were met by the Jewish Agency for Israel, and then flew to Israel, a process known as transmigration.

Initially, a tiny percentage of these émigrés chose to become "dropouts" once they landed in Vienna, expressing a desire to go to another country besides Israel, usually the United States. The Jewish Agency would subsequently refer them to JDC and the Hebrew Immigrant Aid Society (HIAS) for assistance. Dropouts were transported to Ladispoli, near Rome, where HIAS helped them acquire visas and coordinated their resettlement, while JDC provided food and shelter.

Over the course of five years in the first half of the 1970s, the dropout rate, which had been less than 1 percent in 1971, increased dramatically to around 50 percent. The earliest

---

[20] The material in this chapter is drawn from: Hessel, 2007b; Fred A. Lazin, "Refugee Resettlement and 'Freedom of Choice': The Case of Soviet Jewry." *Backgrounder* (Center for Immigration Studies), July, 2005. Retrieved from http://www.cis.org/articles/2005/back705.pdf; and Weiner, 2003.

emigrants possessed a genuine interest in moving to Israel, but many of those who left later obtained visas to Israel because it was the only way they could leave the Soviet Union. The primary intent of the latter group was to escape anti-Semitism and pursue a better economic life in the West.

In addition, life in Israel for Soviet Jews was not always comfortable, at least initially, and intermarried Soviet Jews encountered additional obstacles upon arrival in Israel. The word spread among Soviet Jews that life in the United States was easier than life in Israel, and that Jews who chose the United States would receive support from the U.S. government and from American Jewish federations.

Heated debates ensued among Jewish leaders in the United States and Israel about how to respond to these dropouts. Israeli Prime Minister Golda Meir felt that America was stealing Soviet Jews and tried to stop them from coming to the United States. Others in Israel and the United States who held a parallel pro-Zionist position felt similarly that all Soviet emigrants should go to Israel and advocated an aid cutoff for the dropouts. They offered a number of arguments, maintaining that Soviet Jews would be more likely to remain assimilated if they came to the United States; Israeli visas were being abused; the Soviet Union might decide to rescind emigration altogether; Soviet Jews did not have the status of refugees; and Israel desperately needed the skills of Soviet Jews, since many were highly educated. Also given Arab birthrates, every additional Jew who came to Israel made a demographic difference.

Others, who held a "freedom of choice" perspective, maintained that Jews should be able to live wherever they wished, recalling American restrictions on Jewish immigration during the Nazi era and America's history of welcoming immigrants. They pointed out the unfairness of Soviet emigration policies and the brutal oppression Jews in the Soviet Union had undergone throughout their lives, which had not allowed them the freedom to observe Judaism. Furthermore, if American Jews were not choosing to live in Israel, and if their ancestors had not chosen to live in Israel, on what moral ground could they force Soviet Jews to live there?

Although this passionate debate continued within the organized Jewish community for more than a decade, the discussion never resulted in the threatened aid cutoff. Most American Jews gravitated to the freedom of choice position, since so many were descended from immigrants. Carl Glick of the Hebrew Immigrant Aid Society also made a strong case for the position around the country. Most of the federations and their donors came to embrace this point of view.

In the meantime, the numbers of Soviet Jews who were granted visas to the United States by the American embassy in Rome grew. In 1989, however, at the beginning of the first Bush administration, American policy toward Soviet Jews changed, and a ceiling was placed on the number of Soviet immigrants that could enter the United States.[21] The embassy began rejecting many visa applications, stranding Soviet Jews in Ladispoli. By July 1989, there were 16,000 Soviet Jews under the care of JDC, an increase of over 10,000 in six months.

Even though JDC had not budgeted for this unanticipated situation, it assumed responsibility for the massive expense. In a relatively short period of time, JDC, in the words of then executive vice-president Michael Schneider, began "hemorrhaging...tens and tens of millions of dollars." Dependent as JDC was on the UJA and the federation system, it turned to them for more funding.

Sylvia Hassenfeld, then lay president of JDC, along with Schneider, organized an emergency meeting which was attended by major leaders of Jewish organizations including JDC, the United Jewish Appeal, the Council of Jewish Federations, and the United Israel Appeal. Despite the new needs and budget drain facing JDC, there was considerable resistance to mounting a special fundraising appeal for the Soviet Jews in Ladispoli.

Schneider, who had only recently taken over the leadership

---

21 Joel Brinkley, "Soviet Jews Leave At a Record Pace, Many for Israel." *The New York Times*, December 14, 1989.

post of JDC, recalled that he had been operating under the "naïve assumption" that everyone invited to the table was interested in helping Jews in need. Instead, he came to the unsettling realization that the entire allocation system was driven by ideological considerations.

At the meeting, the Zionist debate position prevailed over the freedom of choice point of view. No additional steps would be taken to provide financial aid to help the dropouts. Despite its obvious budget crisis, JDC was on the wrong side of the issue. Regardless of circumstances on the ground and financial need, when it came to overseas allocations, Schneider observed that the Jewish Agency, representing Israel, was the primary organization in everyone's eyes, while JDC, representing Diaspora Jews, was in distant second place. Schneider worried that the funding system was not flexible enough to respond if another emergency somewhere in the world were to require a dramatic increase in funding.

While JDC did receive a temporary increase in its UJA percentage to address the immediate situation, ultimately, the situation in Ladispoli was resolved through political rather than financial means. Negotiations initiated by Jewish leaders with the State Department, the White House, Congress, and the Immigration and Naturalization Service, as well as Soviet authorities, resulted in Jews obtaining visas in Moscow that allowed them to emigrate directly to the United States. For all practical purposes, the dropout problem was now eliminated. But much bigger challenges were on the horizon for JDC.

JDC Reenters the Soviet Union

The Agro-Joint project that JDC initiated in the 1920s ultimately proved to be a failure. JDC misread the communists, underestimated the dangers, and was forced to cease its operations in the Soviet Union in 1938. Millions of philanthropic dollars were squandered, and many Jews were executed.[22]

---

[22] Sara Kadosh, "American Jewish Joint Distribution Committee," *Encyclopaedia Judaica*. Edited by Michael Berenbaum and Fred Skolnik.

The Soviet government under Stalin viewed religion as an obstacle to the creation of an ideal communist society and suppressed all religious expression. Repression of Judaism intensified and Jewish culture was systematically eradicated. It is estimated that hundreds of thousands of Jews were ultimately murdered and over a million deported to Siberia.

By the 1960s, many Soviet Jews were assimilated and intermarried, and many Jewish schools, organizations, and synagogues were closed or banned. In major cities, only a handful of rabbis remained in state-controlled synagogues that were maintained solely as government showpieces for propaganda purposes.[23] Jews were suspicious of organized religion after years of government indoctrination against it. Any surviving Jewish institutions were viewed as being associated with the government, which the majority of the Soviet population feared and distrusted.

Paralleling the start of Jewish emigration in the late 1960s, Jewish life within the Soviet Union began to reawaken among a segment of Jews who were emboldened by the inspiring success of Israel during the 1967 Six-Day War. A small group covertly began to engage in banned activities, organizing underground Hebrew classes, and arranging for Jewish books to be smuggled in. Within several years, Passover seders began taking place in Moscow, and Jews danced on the streets during *Simchat Torah*.[24] These dissidents gathered on a regular basis to learn more about

---

Volume 2, 2nd edition. Detroit: Macmillan Reference USA, 2007. pages 59-64.

[23] Although Jewish life had virtually ceased in the European areas of the USSR, there were still cities in the Asian republics of the USSR such as Georgia, Uzbekistan, and Azerbaijan that had a thriving Jewish presence.

[24] The Jewish holiday of Passover recalls the biblical exodus of Jews from Egypt. On the first two nights of the holiday, a ceremonial dinner called a seder is held. The Hebrew word seder, which means "order" describes the ritual nature of the meal. The Jewish holiday of Simchat Torah celebrates the completion and beginning of the annual cycle of reading a portion of the Torah – the first five books of the Hebrew Bible – each week. Congregants sing and dance with Torah scrolls.

Judaism as they awaited exit visas for Israel. Young Jews became increasingly identified with Jewish religion and culture.

Under Ralph Goldman, JDC's executive vice-president from 1976 to 1987, JDC supported this rising awareness by smuggling and/or mailing Jewish religious and cultural materials into the Soviet Union. [25] Packages also contained highly sought-after items, such as blue jeans that Jews could sell for income. Goldman, after years of effort, finally received his first official invitation to Moscow from the Soviet Minister of Religious Affairs at the end of 1987.[26] The first JDC delegation visited at the beginning of 1988. The visit was a result of the introduction of *glasnost*[27] by Soviet leader Mikhail Gorbachev, which brought more freedom to Soviet citizens and inspired the creation of a number of local Jewish cultural organizations in communities throughout the Soviet bloc. JDC could now operate more openly.

In May 1989, JDC organized a symposium to plan a strategy for its reentry into the Soviet Union, inviting experts on Soviet Jewry to share their perspectives. The emigration of Soviet Jewry had been the dominant issue to date. Little was understood about the millions of Soviet Jews remaining in the country, who constituted the third largest Jewish population in the world after the United States and Israel. Following the symposium, JDC ended up creating a new Soviet Union Team, which would be led by Michael Schneider, who was now JDC's executive vice-president. The team convened in London and divided up the Soviet Union using a large map. Only one of the six team members knew enough Russian to be able to read it. They had no inkling of what they would encounter and only a small budget to address what they would find.

The team faced two enormous challenges. After decades of systematic repression of Jewish culture and religion, JDC

---

[25] Dr. Saul Cohen served a brief term as executive vice-president of JDC in 1985 and 1986.

[26] Asher Ostrin, "Rebuilding Destroyed Jewish Communities in the FSU," *Journal of Jewish Communal Service*, Fall/Winter 2005, pages 21-23.

[27] Russian for "openness."

would need to figure out how to foster Jewish identity amongst a highly assimilated and intermarried population. And given the lack of synagogues, community centers, Jewish schools, or Jewish leadership, JDC would need to help create viable Jewish institutions in communities across all of the Soviet republics. In determining how to proceed, JDC was severely limited by a small budget and the absence of any fundraising operation. Any new programs would have to be funded at the expense of JDC programs in other countries.

JDC's traditional approach to aid, which had always involved some combination of rescue, relief, and reconstruction/renewal, would have to be adjusted to reflect the stark fiscal realities. Asher Ostrin, a member of the original team who subsequently took over all JDC operations in the Soviet Union, recalls some of the early deliberations:

> *When we first went into the Soviet Union there were two things we were going to stay away from. One was bricks and mortar and the other was welfare....I think in Hungary we were spending somewhere to the tune of $2-2.5 million in welfare and if you extrapolated from that in terms of population size to the Soviet Union it would be completely overwhelming.*[28]

Not only was the cost of welfare prohibitive, the Soviet Union appeared to be taking care of the basic needs of its citizens. JDC decided to focus its initial efforts on renewing Jewish culture and learning, capitalizing on two realities – Soviet citizens were highly literate and read vociferously, and they were not averse to Jewish culture, but rather Jewish religion.

JDC began to translate and distribute Jewish books and establish Jewish libraries. Over a period of several years, it supported Jewish periodicals and performances, Jewish kindergartens, holiday celebrations, and Jewish studies programs in universities. It also worked with local

---

[28]   Asher Ostrin, interview, May 16, 2006.

Jewish cultural organizations that had arisen following the introduction of glasnost.

This was relatively new territory for JDC since its expertise was in saving Jewish lives, not Jewish souls. While these programs were successful and innovative, they received virtually no attention in the United States. American leaders in the Jewish community were preoccupied with Soviet emigration, particularly after the new Bush administration restrictions had just been put into place. During 1989, the first year that JDC began to create programs in the Soviet Union, over 62,500 Soviet Jews left the country, a new emigration record.[29] By this point, only one in every five was choosing Israel as a destination.[30]

The Jewish Agency for Israel had its own Israeli representatives in the Soviet Union to promote emigration to Israel, and JDC's focus on the renewal of Jewish culture and learning drew strong criticism from them. They claimed JDC was obstructing *aliyah*[31] and maintained that its efforts to rebuild Jewish life in the Soviet Union were anti-Zionist.[32] These criticisms came despite public statements by JDC in support of aliyah, and despite the fact that JDC's mission since its founding had been to help Jews in need in their home countries. JDC responded to the criticisms by noting that Soviet Jews who were not currently thinking about emigrating would be more likely to choose to make aliyah if they acquired a Jewish identity through programs like the ones being created, but this argument was ignored. JDC also argued that Soviet Jews had their own economic or personal reasons for staying or leaving, which JDC programs were unlikely to influence.

JDC would focus exclusively on renewal for only a few years. The Soviet economy and political situation were unstable. Glasnost had, for the first time, allowed the Soviet

---

[29] Brinkley, "Soviet Jews Leave."

[30] 12, 932 Soviet Jews emigrated to Israel in 1989; *Jewish Virtual Library*, s.v. "Immigration from the Former Soviet Union," http://www.jewishvirtuallibrary.org/jsource/Immigration/FSU.html.

[31] "Ascent" in Hebrew; the process of emigration to Israel.

[32] Weiner, page 167.

press to expose rampant corruption as well as severe social and economic problems, undermining the Communist Party's power base.

The Collapse of the Soviet Economy

By late 1990, several federations, concerned about reports of Soviet agricultural problems, encouraged JDC to develop a pilot food program. While the focus was intended to be non-sectarian, some of the food would be distributed to Jews. JDC selected Leningrad as the site and relied on hospitals and charitable organizations for distribution. To locate Jews, JDC obtained lists from an Israeli organization that had operated in the Soviet Union since the 1950s, *Lishkat Hakesher*.[33] However, these lists proved inadequate.

With the help of a local woman, JDC was able to identify Jewish names from lists of individuals who were receiving state assistance through a local welfare committee. In this fashion, several hundred elderly Jews who might be potential recipients of food packages were identified. Since Soviet citizens were suspicious of the government, whenever an individual delivering a food package knocked on a door, he or she described the aid package as coming from America. In every case, it was the first time the recipient had ever received anything from the Jewish community. The recipients were intensely grateful and responded in a highly emotional fashion.

From these initial encounters, it became clear that the welfare problem was far larger than anyone had imagined. JDC made arrangements for local Jews to run the Leningrad program and began distributing aid packages in other cities. The logistics of getting the packages into the hands of those who needed them was complicated, since theft was an ever-present possibility. There was a period of trial and error while JDC attempted to establish safe and efficient mechanisms for getting food packages into the right hands.

Simultaneously, JDC was acquiring data about the Soviet

---

[33] Hebrew for "The Liaison Bureau."

Union's Jewish population. JDC learned that Jews in the Soviet Union, unlike Eastern European Jews, were not concentrated in major cities. Stalin had driven Jews into thousands of communities across the various republics. In addition, JDC found that the Jewish population was aging – about one-third were retired individuals living on small pensions. Many had endured great hardship during World War II. Birth rates were low, and there was a great deal of assimilation. Most of the interest in emigration was coming from younger Soviet Jews.

By December 1991, with Gorbachev's power fatally weakened following an August coup attempt, the Soviet Union officially dissolved, its economy in chaos. Food shortages led to rationing for the first time since World War II. There were credible reports of famine, starvation, and food riots. In addition, inflation quickly wiped out the life savings of many elderly Soviet citizens who were living off of their pensions. Hunger in the former Soviet Union was rapidly becoming an international concern. JDC turned out to be one of the few international aid organizations that had any experience with food distribution in the country.

Michael Schneider had been prescient several years earlier when, following the frustrating meetings in search of funding for the Soviet Jews stranded in Ladispoli, he began to wonder how JDC would pay for another crisis. He recalls the period:

> *The Soviet situation exploded, and there again, suddenly we were hit with rapidly expanding need... the more we went into the Soviet Union, the more we realized how vast this problem was going to be.*

Not since World War II had JDC encountered such a large population in need of assistance. In particular, there was an acute need for funding to pay for food. The United Jewish Appeal, which provided virtually all of JDC's funding, would not offer anything remotely close to the amounts that were needed.

Emigration was UJA's overriding and virtually exclusive concern. Through Operation Exodus, UJA would ultimately raise $884 million for Soviet emigration between 1989 and 1994, almost all of which would go to the Jewish Agency for Israel to care for about 750,000 Jewish emigrants from the former Soviet Union. In stark contrast, JDC would receive only about $15 million of this money to address the needs of elderly Soviet Jews who either could not or would not leave.

JDC Responds to the Hunger Crisis

The reports of hunger accompanying the collapse of the former Soviet Union prompted the U.S. House of Representatives to create a task force to investigate. The task force recommended that the U.S. government provide aid through what they termed American private voluntary organizations, acknowledging that it was unlikely that charitable organizations in the FSU could do the job without widespread theft and corruption.

As one of the only American organizations with any experience distributing food in the FSU, JDC was one of the first organizations to apply for a grant from the U.S. Department of Agriculture (USDA). Much to its surprise, it was quickly given $10 million to cover the cost of over a half-million food parcels for Jews and non-Jews, plus another $4 million for shipping and distribution.

Although the task was monumental, JDC was able to deliver the parcels with virtually no shrinkage. Not only was the USDA impressed by the result, the entire process provided JDC with valuable contacts in the FSU and ample experience with logistics. The experience also generated a great deal of goodwill for the organization among both Jews and non-Jews, and gave the Soviet Union Team its first large-scale success.

JDC's accomplishment was, however, only an initial step, since JDC's policy throughout its history was not to be a welfare agency but to create local Jewish welfare institutions that could eventually become self-sufficient. Creating these institutions would be a considerable challenge in the FSU, where the concept of welfare was not viewed in a positive light, there was no tradition of volunteerism, Jewish traditions were largely unknown, and independent agencies could potentially be exploited by corrupt officials.

Over time, despite these obstacles, JDC staff member Amos Avgar developed what was to become known as the Hesed model, a community-based organization that provided a variety of Jewish-themed services to the Jewish elderly in communities throughout the FSU.[34] These included hot meals, medical care, clothing and fuel, personal grooming services, and cultural programming. Services were provided in local homes and at cheerfully decorated community centers, the latter a dramatic, deliberately chosen contrast to the typical drab, poorly lit facilities that had been the prevailing model during the Soviet era.

Funding to support the nascent Hesed center initiative came from an unexpected source, an "extremely colorful character"[35] named Larry Rochlin. Rochlin was a Russian-speaking Polish Jew who had fought in the Polish army in exile under General Wladyslaw Anders during World War II.[36] Rochlin, who was based in Reno, Nevada, was seeking worthwhile philanthropic causes to support and learned about JDC's new efforts in the former Soviet Union. Since he was interested in the elderly, following a meeting with Asher Ostrin of JDC, he decided to support the newly emerging Hesed centers. Although no formal fundraising effort took place on the part of JDC to acquire the money, once again JDC had obtained outside money from sources other than its traditional funders. However, even with the successes of the USDA grant and Rochlin donation, the enormous numbers of Jewish elderly in need of food required much more support.

In 1992, following the reunification of Germany, money became available under the auspices of the Claims Conference from the sale of pre-World War II Jewish property in East Germany. The Claims Conference originated in 1952 when a

---

[34] See Amos Avgar, Roni Kaufman, Leonid Kolton, and Sofia Abramova, "The Hesed Welfare Model," *Journal of Jewish Communal Service*, Winter/Spring 2003, pages 125-130. The program has now grown to serve 180,000 Jews in 2,922 locations.

[35] Asher Ostrin, e-mail correspondence, January 3, 2008.

[36] For the full story of the Polish army in exile, see Anders, 1949.

group of representatives of Jewish organizations met with the government of West Germany to obtain reparations for the damages and destruction experienced by Jews at the hands of the Nazi regime.[37]

Up to this point in time, the Claims Conference had provided reparation money to individual survivors, and had funded capital projects for survivors, such as old age homes and nursing homes, but had not provided support for other types of programs. Given the newly available money from East Germany, Michael Schneider and JDC staff began to make the case to the Claims Conference that Jews in the former Soviet Union constituted a special situation that required a new set of policies.

The process of obtaining approval took several years, but in the fall of 1995 the Claims Conference agreed to start providing substantial sums of money for Holocaust survivors and Nazi victims in the FSU, which would be administered through the Hesed centers under the supervision and guidance of JDC. JDC's welfare budget, set previously in the vicinity of half a million dollars a year, suddenly jumped to $18 million (see Table A2 in Appendix A for a historical perspective on JDC's budget for the former Soviet Union).

The new money, although badly needed, made things even more complicated for JDC. Claims money could be used only for direct services to Holocaust survivors and Nazi victims. JDC would need to find additional money to cover Hesed center administrative costs. It would also need funding to provide comparable welfare services to non-survivors who were struggling under virtually identical circumstances but could not benefit from the new funding. Fortunately, JDC was able to obtain $2 million for this purpose from the Harry and Jeannette Weinberg Foundation of Baltimore.

Harry Weinberg's relationship with JDC had begun some years earlier in the summer of 1988 when he and Darrell Friedman, who was then president of the Baltimore federation,

---

[37] For additional information about the Conference on Jewish Material Claims Against Germany, see http://www.claimscon.org. For a comprehensive history, see Henry, 2007.

went on a UJA mission to Israel. Weinberg, who had acquired much of his fortune through Hawaiian real estate holdings, had a strong interest in supporting the elderly. He asked Friedman to arrange a visit to a home for the aged in Israel, specifically so that he could spend time with residents to learn first-hand about the quality of their care. To organize the visit, Friedman reached out to an old friend, Zvi Feine, who worked for JDC-Israel.

Feine brought Weinberg and Friedman to a home for the aged in the town of Rishon Letzion, where, in the summer's heat, it was readily apparent that the facility was not air-conditioned. On the spot, Weinberg pledged a $1 million gift to provide air-conditioning to every old-age home in Israel.

Weinberg died several years later, but his foundation continued his work and elected to support JDC's programs for the elderly in the former Soviet Union. In the process of obtaining this outside funding, along with the funding from Rochlin, JDC gained experience that would prove invaluable for attracting new donors and set the stage for the creation of its own fundraising operation a few years later.

By the mid 1990s, in response to urgent needs, JDC had managed to acquire some of the funding it needed to support welfare programs in the former Soviet Union. In contrast with its previous stance, the Jewish Agency for Israel approved of JDC's programs for the elderly, recognizing that Israel simply could not address the needs of these Jews if they were to emigrate to Israel. The expense of caring for large numbers of elderly Soviet Jews could cripple the Israeli economy.

As JDC gained fundraising experience, the existing funding system that had supported JDC since 1939 underwent a transformation. Donor mindsets began to change, and the federation system became increasingly unhappy with the way the United Jewish Appeal was disbursing the money it raised.

Chapter 3: New Trends in Giving and Spending

Allocations for Overseas Needs Decline

When the United Jewish Appeal was established just prior to World War II to raise money for overseas Jewry, it essentially brought to an end the multiple-agency approach to fundraising that had dominated the landscape. The subsequent creation of the State of Israel generated even more unity, and the United Jewish Appeal brought in ever-increasing amounts thereafter. Crises in Israel, specifically the 1967 and 1973 wars, generated huge jumps in fundraising revenues, which did not revert back to previous levels once the crises ended.

For a number of years after UJA was created, there were two fundraising campaigns in each Jewish community that had a federation, one by the local federation to meet the local needs of the community, and one by UJA for overseas needs. Eventually, community by community, these campaigns merged. Federations then assumed responsibility for both local and overseas needs through their annual campaigns. Each local federation kept a portion of the money it raised each year to be disbursed to programs and institutions in its community and gave the rest to UJA for overseas needs. UJA continued to fundraise in smaller Jewish communities where there were no federations.

As a result of these mergers, UJA's role shifted from fundraising to advocacy on behalf of JDC and the United Israel Appeal. UJA sought to obtain the highest possible amount for overseas needs from each community. While the amounts and percentages that were spent locally or sent overseas differed at each federation, UJA, under the forceful and innovative leadership of Rabbi Herbert Friedman, was highly effective at inspiring donors by emphasizing the importance of supporting Israel. On average, 50 percent or more of federation campaign money was allocated overseas nationally from the time of the Six-Day War in 1967 through the late 1980s.

Even though most of the United Jewish Appeal's funding came from the federations, UJA was legally owned by the two American organizations that it was originally created to raise funds for, the United Israel Appeal (UIA), which supported the Jewish Agency for Israel (JAFI), and the American Jewish Joint Distribution Committee.[38]

UJA operated independently of the Council of Jewish Federations and had its own budget.[39] The major advantage of this funding system was that it freed JAFI and JDC from fundraising responsibilities and allowed them to focus entirely on their core missions. From JDC's perspective, the arrangement worked, as described by Steve Schwager, JDC's current executive vice-president and chief executive officer: "[The arrangement] allowed JDC the ability to be creative and innovative and risk taking because it didn't have to worry about resources."[40]

When UJA was founded, it was agreed that the money UJA received from federation campaigns would be split according to a formula negotiated by UIA and JDC. During World War II and immediately thereafter, JDC received the largest share, but once the State of Israel was created, UIA became the primary recipient.

From the very start of the United Jewish Appeal, the formula was a source of contention. The degree of conflict over the formula grew or diminished at various points in time. For example, in the late 1970s and early 1980s, the lay leaders of JDC

---

[38] Because of United States tax laws, the Jewish Agency for Israel could not raise money directly in the United States.

[39] In the mid-1990s, UJA had an annual administrative budget of $25 million, while the Council of Jewish Federations had a budget of $11 million.

[40] Steve Schwager, interview, August 14, 2006.

and the United Israel Appeal were good friends. They came to an agreement between themselves and essentially shook hands on it. At other times, discussions were so contentious that the Council of Jewish Federations needed to intervene as a third party to settle matters. Each organization wore a public face of cooperation, but behind the scenes the battles were fierce. Each side had its own forceful rationale and ideology for increasing its share of overseas allocations from federations.

JDC's focus was on helping Jews around the world. JDC funds supported social and welfare programs that aided hundreds of thousands of Jews in distress. Without its help, many remote Jewish communities would simply not be able to survive. JDC maintained that Jews should be able to live wherever they wished and that all Jews were responsible for one another.

The United Israel Appeal argued on behalf of the Jewish Agency for Israel that Israel should be the main recipient of funds since a strong Jewish homeland was essential to the survival of the Jewish people. Furthermore, the UIA felt strongly that Jews who were in distress should move to Israel instead of staying in their home countries and relying on JDC support. Life in their home countries was unstable at best, and for them to remain was not in the best interests of the Jewish people. Spending money on Jews in these countries, UIA argued, was not a wise use of resources. [41]

When Ralph Goldman served as the executive vice-president of JDC in the 1970s and 1980s, he argued for a 50/50 formula based on parity between the two organizations. His view did not prevail. By the mid-1980s, the process of negotiating the formula became more structured and formalized, involving meetings between teams of two or three individuals who represented each agency and negotiated a formula every few years.

In the late 1980s, the Jewish Agency for Israel was subjected to enormous financial pressures as a consequence of Soviet emigration and went into deep debt, creating even more tension

---

[41]   Kolker, 2005.

over the split. During the period of greatest Soviet emigration to Israel, beginning in 1989, the two agencies settled on a 77/23 formula, with the larger percentage going to UIA for JAFI. JAFI needed every possible dollar, despite the supplementary federation support it was receiving from Project Exodus that would eventually amount to almost $1 billion.

However, beginning in the late 1980s, the combined amount of allocations from all federations for overseas needs began to decline, threatening funding for both JAFI and JDC (see Table A3 in Appendix A for a historical overview of overseas allocations from the federation system). Total allocations for overseas needs to UJA peaked at $368 million in 1987 ($663 million in present-day dollars), with 50.4 percent of total federation campaign money allocated for overseas needs. The trend from this point on was downward. By 2000, the percentage of federation campaign money allocated for overseas needs was only 33 percent, a decline of $95 million from 1987.

No single event or trend was responsible for this decline. Rather, a combination of forces contributed. For most of the 20th century, the federation fundraising model operated under the principle that the leadership of the Jewish community was in the best position to determine where needs were greatest and where federation funds should be spent. Unity was the dominant theme – donors were exhorted to give to their fellow Jews and trust that the money would be allocated wisely. Unrestricted giving was a virtue. Designated or "earmarked" giving was something to be avoided. This model, known as the collective responsibility approach, began to erode in the 1990s on a number of fronts. Changes began taking place at multiple levels – among American Jewry as a whole, federation leaders, and individual donors.

Unrest Among the Federations

In 1990, as it had twenty years earlier, the Council of Jewish Federations conducted a survey to learn more about the characteristics of American Jewry. When the report of the National

Jewish Population Survey was released in June 1991, its impact was nothing short of alarming. The data collected in 1970 indicated that among Jews who married prior to 1965, only nine percent married individuals who were not Jewish. However, for the period from 1986 to 1990, the newer findings showed that 52 percent were marrying non-Jews, more than a five-fold increase.[42]

Almost instantly, interest in the security of Israel and the emigration of Soviet Jewry was superseded by concerns about the future of Jewish life in America. Previous data revealed that intermarried couples were less likely to raise their children as Jews than in-married couples. Federations, almost frantically, began to focus on community-based "Jewish continuity" programs designed to influence the next generation to grow up to make Jewish choices and raise Jewish children. This meant that some of the federation campaign money that had previously gone to the United Jewish Appeal was now being allocated for local programs.

Battles ensued in a number of communities, but UJA was unable to overcome this new trend among federations. Steve Schwager describes UJA at the time as "... a paper tiger...it could scream and it could yell but it had no effective means of getting federations to do anything."

Just as the UJA was frustrated by its inability to influence federation decisions, federation executives were frustrated about the way that UJA was operating. They were faithfully paying into the system but had no input into the decisions that were being made regarding the overseas programs and agencies their allocations were supporting. Lee Wunsch, executive for the Jewish Federation of Greater Houston, recalls the prevailing sentiment: "We basically were writing a check

---

[42] Several years later, the validity of the 52 percent intermarriage rate finding and its implications for Jewish continuity were questioned. However, in 1991, when the study was issued, the figure was assumed to be accurate, and the Jewish community responded to the problem accordingly. See Stephen M. Cohen, "Why Intermarriage May Not Threaten Jewish Continuity," *Moment*, June 1994.

to UJA and…we didn't know what was going on. There was no transparency in the system."[43]

Furthermore, the executives did not have any say regarding the formula for the split between JDC and UIA. Their problem was not with JDC, whose work on behalf of world Jewry they respected. Even though they had almost no direct contact with JDC, they viewed it as a kindred organization and a natural partner. In essence, JDC was supporting the same types of welfare programs overseas that the federations were supporting in their local communities. JDC operated with an American sensibility, professionalism, and transparency.

The federation executives did, however, have serious concerns about the United Israel Appeal and the Jewish Agency for Israel. While many of the Jewish Agency's programs were important and vital for the Jewish people, the Jewish Agency itself was viewed as bureaucratic, disorganized, and unresponsive. Decisions regarding the use of funds were made by Israeli political appointees, not professionals, and the organization incurred excessive amounts of debt.[44]

Federations also did not share the perspective of JAFI, which viewed funds raised in the United States by the federations and allocated for use in Israel as the equivalent of a tax on Americans. JAFI used American funds for current needs, even when these needs were not part of its central mission. In addition, JAFI's accounting was not conducted according to American standards, and the ensuing lack of transparency raised questions. Even though there were some federation executives on the JAFI Board of Governors, they had little influence. The prevailing sentiment was that the federations' fiduciary responsibility to their donors required more oversight of JAFI than was currently the case.[45]

---

[43] Lee Wunsch, interview, June 28, 2007.

[44] See Hoffman, 1989.

[45] Historian Jonathan Sarna draws a distinction between what he calls a stewardship view of money, which focuses on accountability and transparency, and an instrumental view of money, which views financial resources as a means to help others, with less concern for how the money is managed. These two perspectives neatly correspond to the JDC and JAFI approaches to the use of philanthropic dollars. The

Moreover, as fears for Israel's survival ebbed, there was a greater willingness to challenge JAFI.

Eventually, these concerns reached a boiling point. In 1993, the executives of a number of large-city federations sent a letter to the leadership of UJA and CJF suggesting it was time to explore the "structure, governance and accountability" of the two agencies.[46] A study group was subsequently commissioned to analyze the situation. This heralded the beginnings of the process that led to the eventual dissolution of both organizations in 1999, when the United Jewish Communities was created.

Starting a decade before the creation of the study group, several federations had begun to develop direct relationships with overseas agencies, bypassing the United Jewish Appeal. The first to do so was San Francisco. In 1984, San Francisco federation executive Brian Lurie started an Israel advisory board, which was given $100,000 to spend on projects of its own choosing. Later, other federations began to defect from the existing overseas allocation system in small but significant ways. While not withholding money from UJA outright, federations in communities such as Boston, Cleveland, Los Angeles, and Minneapolis subsequently made decisions not to give all of their overseas allocations to UJA as they had in the past. Rather, they too chose to bypass UJA and give money from annual campaigns directly to JDC, JAFI, and other overseas agencies in support of specific projects.

A New Donor Mindset[47]

The desire on the part of federations to divert overseas allocations from UJA was motivated not just by dissatisfaction

---

author thanks Professor Sarna for his helpful comments regarding this distinction.

[46] Larry Yudelson, "CJF, UJA Launch Study That May Lead to New Jewish Fund-Raising Structure," *Jewish Telegraph Agency*, April 27, 1994.

[47] Portions of this section draw upon Jack Wertheimer, "Politics and Jewish Giving," *Commentary*, December 1997, pages 32-36.

with UJA, UIA, and JAFI. Federations also wanted to interest current donors and new donors in compelling overseas projects that might inspire them to give.

This process had to occur carefully. There was no benefit to a federation if a current donor simply shifted his or her donation from the annual campaign to an overseas project. Rather, the intent was for a donor to maintain his or her level of unrestricted annual giving while supplementing it with a designated gift.

Creating direct connections to overseas projects might have the effect of inspiring donors who were previously not inclined to give to federations at all. Federation executives could see that donor mindsets were changing. The notion of undesignated giving to a general fund like a federation campaign was becoming less appealing. Donors wanted to become more involved with recipient organizations. They wanted to give to specific causes that were meaningful to them and become directly involved with those who were benefiting from their giving. Giving was not merely seen as a Jewish obligation, but increasingly a form of personal expression. As a consequence, designated giving was on the rise. John Ruskay, executive for the UJA-Federation of New York, describes the trends among donors:

> *We the federations are now against the grain. Said differently, we are a Jewish philanthropic mutual fund at a time when increasingly people want to select their own philanthropic stock. This is a result of what I refer to as 'rampant individualism' which impacts all of American culture, including philanthropy. Increasingly, people want to do their own philanthropic thing.*[48]

At the same time, the traditional federation donor base was aging. Giving to Israel and other Jewish causes was automatic for those who had memories of the horrors of World War II

---

[48]   John Ruskay, interview, March 30, 2007.

and the five subsequent wars fought by the State of Israel. For baby boomers, however, these were not personal memories. They were merely historical facts and did not have the same visceral impact. Younger donors were less inclined to give to Jewish organizations and more interested in secular social, political, environmental, or humanitarian causes. One Jewish fundraiser humorously observed that if younger donors were presented with a choice between helping fellow Jews or saving whales, "the whales win."

Those who did give to Jewish causes were increasingly inclined to give directly, rather than through a federation. As a result, federation campaigns were becoming dominated by a smaller core of older donors. These donors on average were giving more than they had in the past, but overall, fewer people were giving to federations. The mass philanthropy approach that developed during World War I, in which every Jew gave something to help his or her fellow Jew, was now eroding.

Family foundations also began to emerge around this time. Wealthy donors began to create their own foundations instead of giving money to federations. They wanted to make their own decisions about where to spend their money. Federations were increasingly seen as slow, unresponsive, and bureaucratic. Through family foundations, donors could act decisively, unencumbered by committees and deliberations.

These tendencies were further influenced by the policies of President Ronald Reagan, who saw "big government" as the problem and market forces and entrepreneurship as the solution. Federations had begun to acquire a negative, "big government" image. A new "venture philanthropy" model began to enter Jewish life.

Policies and trends in Israel also contributed to the decline in overseas giving. Right-leaning policies promulgated by Israeli politicians during the 1990s alienated a segment of America's liberal Jews, who spoke out against the United Jewish Appeal and its unquestioning pro-Israel orientation. These Jews were concerned that money would be going to the right-wing Orthodox in Israel, which was anathema to them.

Furthermore, not only was aliyah declining in the 1990s, but Israel's thriving economy and engagement in the Oslo peace initiative gave the illusion that the country had a secure and prosperous future. Consequently, the sense of urgency regarding giving to Israel was diminished.

The fundamental problem the entire national federation system was facing was that there was no single compelling overseas cause to capture the hearts and checkbooks of donors as had been the case in the past. Local needs were seen by donors and federations as more pressing.

JDC Faces a Major Budget Shortfall

The decline in UJA revenues in the 1990s meant that there was less available for JDC. In 1994, JDC presented UJA with an annual budget of $90 million, which included all of the new expenses associated with addressing the needs of the elderly in the former Soviet Union. The United Israel Appeal and the Jewish Agency were still under enormous financial pressure from Soviet emigration. They were unwilling to consider any changes in the previous 77/23 formula that would reduce their allocation.

The Council of Jewish Federations had to intervene in the negotiations. The new agreement that was finally settled upon shifted the formula slightly in JDC's favor and provided for a one-time $15 million grant from Operation Exodus.[49] JDC would now be receiving an annual average allocation of about $67 million, which was still $23 million less than their projected needs.

Within a few years, JDC would establish a fundraising department to address the shortfall. It had operated successfully without one since 1939, when UJA was created.

---

[49] JDC has pointed out that this represented less than two percent of the funds raised through Operation Exodus for Soviet Jews, even though JDC was attempting to serve the needs of as many as 1.5 million Jews in the former Soviet Union, roughly equal to the number of emigrants that the Jewish Agency was serving. JAFI contends that the money was collected specifically for Operation Exodus, not for welfare.

PART 2: JDC RESPONDS TO THE CHANGING ENVIRONMENT

Chapter 4: A New Resource Development Program

Executive in Residence

Alan Gill had served as the federation executive in Columbus, Ohio for eight years when he made arrangements to spend an exploratory year in Israel with his family to see if it would be feasible to make aliyah. They arrived in Israel in the summer of 1992.

Once he settled in, Gill explored various options about how to spend his time in Israel. When he approached Michael Schneider about a part-time, unpaid arrangement with JDC, Schneider said yes almost immediately. Schneider later attributed the decision to "chemistry." He sensed that Gill's federation experience would be helpful to JDC-Israel and that he was a good fit for the organization's unique culture. They decided on an amorphous title for Gill, "executive in residence."

Gill spent his initial months meeting JDC-Israel staff and learning about its programs and philosophy. JDC-Israel had evolved over the years into a sophisticated and highly-respected agency that piloted cutting-edge social service programs in partnership with the government of Israel. It also implemented new program initiatives for the elderly, disabled, children-at-risk, new immigrants, and the unemployed. Pilot initiatives that proved to be successful were subsequently taken over by the Israeli government.

JDC-Israel drew about one-third of JDC's total global budget, which was supplemented by small grants from American foundations and larger grants from the Israeli government.

JDC also had a research arm in Israel that conducted social science research on Israeli society, which at the time was known as the JDC-Brookdale Institute.[50] One conversation with Jack Habib, director of the institute, captured Gill's attention. Gill learned from Habib that a new research study found that most of the Soviet Jews who emigrated to Israel obtained full-time employment.

Gill recognized that this information had significant public relations value for JDC. Federations had taken on a considerable financial burden to fund Soviet emigration and were justifiably concerned that they might have to continue providing support for Soviet émigrés once these Jews had settled in Israel. The research instead showed that Soviet Jews were becoming self-supporting. Gill knew that this information would be welcome news to federations and disseminated the information among his federation colleagues.

Prior to Gill's arrival, direct contact between JDC-Israel and federation leaders was rare. The relationship JDC-Israel had with federation executive Darrell Friedman of Baltimore, which led to the funding from the Weinberg Foundation, was the exception rather than the rule. This lack of contact was understandable since UJA had been responsible for advocating on JDC's behalf with federations, allowing JDC to focus its total energies on serving Jews in need. Gill recognized that the best use of his time during the exploratory year was to work on establishing connections with federations and foundations. There were a number of federation and foundation executives who were not even aware that JDC operated in Israel. Over the years, the United Jewish Appeal fostered the impression that JAFI was synonymous with Israel and JDC with Diaspora Jewry, perceptions that were no longer accurate. UJA also presented

---

50 In 2004, the JDC-Brookdale Institute became known as the Myers-JDC-Brookdale Institute when it received a $15 million endowment from the Cleveland-based David and Inez Myers Foundation.

JDC programs to federations in an oversimplified fashion that did not give them a proper sense of JDC's global reach.

Gill also saw the need to educate JDC's management about the changes he saw taking place in the federation system. Although JDC did engage in strategic planning, JDC was strictly concerned with trends that might have an effect on its programs around the world. JDC was not looking at philanthropic trends in the United States that might affect its funding. Michael Schneider's focus was on international Jewry rather than the federation world. He recognized and respected Gill's perspective.

Gill highlighted four important trends that he believed would have a significant impact on JDC and shared these "future headlines" with Schneider and senior JDC staff. First, he described the declining influence of the United Jewish Appeal in the federation system and predicted the eventual demise of the organization. Gill argued that JDC needed to find its own voice in the federation system instead of relying exclusively on UJA to make the case for its programs.

Second, Gill pointed out to JDC that some federations had begun to bypass the existing funding system and were giving a portion of the money from their annual campaigns directly to agencies in Israel. Gill predicted that even more federations would follow. UJA was fighting to prevent this from occurring but was likely to lose the battle since it no longer had the power to influence federation decisions regarding overseas allocations. Even though the trend toward more designated funding by federations appeared to be problematic for JDC, since money was being diverted from JDC's undesignated funding, Gill maintained that JDC needed to be "ahead of the curve" and proactive in positioning itself to obtain this new resource stream. Otherwise the money would simply end up going to other agencies.[51]

Third, Gill noted that federations were beginning to shift away

---

[51] JDC currently receives $34 million annually in designated funding from federations. It did not receive any designated funding from federations in 1996. See Chapter 7.

from sending money overseas and were increasingly focused on domestic programs that would enhance Jewish continuity. This trend did not bode well for overseas allocations in the future.

Fourth, Gill made the case to JDC that it had to look beyond the federation system altogether. As a former federation executive, he knew all too well there were many wealthy Jewish donors that federations were failing to reach. He believed that JDC, if it were to adopt the right approaches, might be able to access this untapped source of funding since its programs could inspire giving if donors knew more about them.

Toward the end of his exploratory year, Gill, working closely with Sara Hirschhorn and Jack Habib at JDC, organized a seminar for federation executives and lay leaders at JDC-Israel, the first of its type ever held. Over the course of two days, in partnership with JDC-Israel staff, Gill, Habib, and Hirschhorn took these leaders to visit program sites in Israel and arranged discussion groups so that they would become more familiar with JDC. The event was highly successful and greatly appreciated by the federation leaders who participated. It was an eye-opener, since few of them had encountered first-hand JDC programs in Israel and the Israelis their overseas allocations were supporting.

Soon after the seminar, in September 1993, Gill became a full-time employee of JDC. He and his family decided to make aliyah. For the next few years, with the full support of Michael Schneider, Gill worked on marketing JDC-Israel directly to federations and foundations so that the organization could position itself to be the beneficiary of emerging trends. He arranged meetings with federation executives when they came through Israel, a time that allowed for relaxed and productive conversations uninterrupted by local concerns. He also arranged for them to visit JDC programs in the former Soviet Union. Since the focus of the federations had been exclusively on emigration from the former Soviet Union, it was enlightening for them to see what JDC was doing for the 1.5 million Jews who had chosen to remain in their homeland.

New Board President, New Fundraising Approaches

Throughout its history, JDC had an elite board. Membership was considered highly prestigious. Board members consisted of some of the most generous, successful, and dedicated leaders among American Jewry. JDC staff member Vivian Green describes the process of becoming a member:

> *Board members were largely nominated through recommendations from their federations and then approved by JDC. Nominees were leaders and major donors in their communities. Being a member of the JDC board has always been regarded as sort of a plum...it was a reward for community giving and active leadership at a federation.* [52]

The presidency of the JDC board was anything but ceremonial. The position was extremely demanding, involving frequent travel at the board president's own expense to countries that JDC served all over the world. Presidents were carefully selected by a nominating committee after 5 to 10 years of demonstrated leadership as the chair of several key board committees, and after having visited many of the countries served by JDC.

In the fall of 1996, Jonathan Kolker was nominated for board president following his roles as treasurer, chair of the Africa and Asia Committee, and chair of the Budget and Finance Committee. Kolker, a highly successful real estate developer from Baltimore, previously served as president of the Baltimore federation and joined the JDC board some years earlier in the same way that most other board members joined, through a nomination by his federation for exemplary service.

To prepare for his new role as president, Kolker spent a day that fall with Michael Schneider on the balcony of a Jerusalem hotel. The two men discussed what they felt JDC's priorities and policies should be for the four years of Kolker's term.

---

[52] Vivian Green, interview, May 4, 2006.

Much of the conversation involved reviewing JDC's current challenges in the former Soviet Union. Given the hundreds of thousands of elderly Jews who had been identified as needing support, and the equally large number who were clamoring for programs to help them reconnect with Jewish tradition, JDC staff estimated that the organization would need to increase its revenues by an additional $90 million a year. Of that figure, $60 million would be spent on welfare programs, and $30 million on Jewish renewal programs. The only alternative would be to ignore the massive hunger – both for food and for Judaism – and withhold services.

It was clear that little, if any of the additional money needed was going to come from UJA and the federation system. Kolker describes the reality at the time:

> *The federations really were unable to respond. They had just completed these two Exodus campaigns [for Soviet Jews]; they had harvested the American Jewish community for these huge amounts of additional gifts. People were doubling and tripling their gift to pay for [Operation] Exodus. Exodus was paying for aliyah. There wasn't any energy, there wasn't any money, there wasn't any enthusiasm for another campaign.[53]*

Over the course of the day's discussion, Kolker and Schneider formulated a five-part strategy to increase JDC revenues:
- JDC would attempt to expand its advocacy efforts with the United Jewish Appeal and the federation system, recognizing that this would at best generate only a fraction of the amounts needed.
- JDC would create an entirely new resource development program that would not compete with federation and UJA fundraising.
- JDC would seek to increase the Holocaust restitution funding it had already started receiving for Jews in

---

[53] Jonathan Kolker, interview, January 31, 2007.

the former Soviet Union using several arguments: a) these Jews were double victims of both Nazism and Communism; b) they had not previously received restitution funds; c) they lived in a country where social services were virtually non-existent and were the neediest of Holocaust survivors; d) unlike Holocaust survivors in the United States and Israel, they had no organizations to advocate on their behalf.

- JDC would attempt to transfer funds budgeted for other countries serviced by JDC without reducing services to the Jews of these countries.
- JDC would search for other funding sources.[54]

Prior to establishing the new resource development program, JDC had only one staff member based in New York who was responsible for relationships with donors. Despite the lack of a formal fundraising department, JDC had received several million dollars a year in donations. In the words of Alan Gill, much of the money "just fell in our lap."[55]

The donations originated from two sources. Because JDC helped hundreds of thousands of Jews over the course of its history, particularly during and after World War II, it regularly received unsolicited checks in the mail as well as bequests when someone died. There were also a few donations from members of JDC's board. However, JDC had no financial expectations of its board members. Unlike virtually all other nonprofits, JDC never viewed its board as a financial resource. Board members were only expected to give to their local federations. Kolker would attempt to change this board philosophy over the course of his tenure.

Ground Rules for Fundraising

---

[54] Jonathan Kolker, "The Creation of a Resource Development Program at JDC in Response to the Unprecedented Relief and Renewal Needs of the Jews Remaining in the Former Soviet Union (1997-2000)," January 31, 2003. Internal memo, JDC.

[55] Alan Gill, interview, May 4, 2006.

Considering its history and culture, the decision to start what JDC would call a resource development program, while a dire necessity, was still a significant shift for JDC. The initiative was further complicated by political realities that constrained JDC from using the fundraising approaches that other Jewish organizations employed. As JDC's primary source of funding came from the federation system, JDC could not antagonize federations by competing with them directly for donors and donations. The federations were partners in helping JDC do its work, and JDC was the overseas arm of the federation system. JDC simply could not divert dollars from annual campaigns.

Practically speaking, this meant that JDC would not be able to employ such standard fundraising practices as advertisements or direct mail campaigns because these would tread too heavily on federation turf. The dilemma faced by Kolker and Schneider was to devise a way to raise substantial amounts of money for JDC from those Jewish donors who were already inclined to give money to overseas Jewish causes, but without threatening federation revenues.

Given these constraints, the two men formulated a strategy with firm ground rules designed to maintain goodwill with federations. JDC would limit its fundraising focus to a select group of a few hundred wealthy donors who could afford to give substantial amounts to JDC in addition to their federation contributions. The JDC board would be enlisted to identify and help cultivate these donors. JDC would inform local federations prior to contacting these potential donors and would not accept money from a donor if the gift were to adversely affect the donor's existing contribution to the federation's annual campaign.

Kolker and Schneider decided that JDC would seek donations of $1 million or greater, with a minimum threshold of $250,000. Donors offering less would be told to give the money to their local federation. JDC would subsequently be criticized by some for having an elitist fundraising strategy, but the strategy in its view was conceived in response to the unique circumstances it faced.

JDC had now established a fundraising department, but the department was sui generis. It would take a singular individual to direct it, because whoever took on the position would have to operate it "with one hand tied behind his back," in the words of Michael Schneider.

JDC did not have to look far for a director. Kolker's first act as president of the board in December 1996 was to approve Michael Schneider's recommendation to appoint Alan Gill. Gill was a "perfect choice" according to Kolker, for two reasons:

> *First of all, as the exec. in Columbus, he had fundraising experience, and two, he was sensitive to the concerns of the federations....JDC would be competing with them for funds. We knew that Alan would not cross the line of allowing our fundraising efforts, our resource development efforts, to negatively impact the federations. As a prior exec., he knew where the line was.*

Gaining the Support of the Federations and the United Israel Appeal

Gaining federation and UIA support for the new fundraising initiatives would be crucial for JDC's success. In February 1997, Schneider attended a meeting in Boca Raton, Florida with the executives of the largest federations to have a frank conversation about JDC's situation in the former Soviet Union and inform them about its new fundraising strategies.

Schneider first discussed the national funding system for overseas needs, and made the case, as he had repeatedly since first becoming executive vice-president, that the funding system should not be driven by ideology, as it currently was, but rather by needs. The system was too inflexible and unable to respond in a timely fashion to rapidly changing realities. The current allocations procedure, which involved having representatives from the United Israel Appeal and JDC sit down and hammer out a formula every few years, simply was not working. The federation executives themselves would need to play an active role in coming up with a new way to allocate money between JDC and JAFI. Schneider's polemic fell on sympathetic ears since federation executives already shared these sentiments, and had already been meeting to revamp the system. Several years later, when the United Jewish Communities came into existence, it would attempt to actualize Schneider's vision.

Schneider then described the situation in the Soviet Union. Following his presentation, Steven Nasatir, the federation executive from Chicago, put forward a plan for a special two-year, $10 million per year advance from the federations to JDC which would be funded from future increases to annual campaign revenues.[56] The federations had heard Schneider and were making a good faith effort to help JDC pay for its new programs in the former Soviet Union.

In addition to Schneider's meeting with the federation executives, both Schneider and Kolker spent the first six months of 1997 traveling around the United States to meet with lay and professional leadership at the twenty largest federations. They described the challenges JDC faced in the former Soviet Union and explained their new fundraising strategy. The intent was twofold. They were looking for additional financial support, and they wanted to defuse any potential backlash from federations regarding JDC's new resource development department. Kolker describes the result of these visits: "In some cases, we actually got direct funding...but in all cases, virtually all cases, they understood our valid reason for opening a resource development department, and they didn't undermine it or object to it and kill it."

Beyond the federations, Kolker and Schneider also needed to make sure that the United Israel Appeal and the Jewish Agency for Israel would not object to their new fundraising initiative. At a meeting with UIA representatives, they negotiated an agreement whereby they would be able to raise money from

---

[56] The plan ultimately yielded about $14 million over two years, since not all of the federations paid into it.

other sources as long as their efforts did not have an adverse impact on UIA revenues.

A Green Seder Plate

Following the launch of the new resource development department, Kolker and Schneider began to identify prospects. As Kolker recalls, JDC board members were an obvious target, since "one of the cardinal rules of fundraising is you go to your board first." However, at the time, board members were not expected to contribute to JDC – they were only expected to give to their local federation. Getting them to contribute to JDC would require a change in the board's culture.

A study in 1996 found that JDC board members gave an average of $200,000 to their local federation, so it was clear that board members had the capacity to give to JDC. Just what would it take to encourage them to give? Kolker decided that as the board president he would need to set an example, and made a personal commitment to contribute $1 million. He then approached JDC's five living past presidents and obtained seven-figure commitments from each.

The six became the first members of the new JDC Warburg Society, which would consist of board members who pledged in excess of $250,000. The Warburg Society was created to recognize the generosity of board members, and it was only appropriate for there to be a tangible gift of appreciation. The dilemma was finding a suitable choice. Kolker recalls the challenge: "We are soliciting Bronfmans and Tischs...they have got Picassos on their walls...we are not going to find anything at Tiffany's that is going to interest them."

Around that time, while visiting the Holocaust Museum in Washington, DC, Kolker spotted a green, glazed earthenware seder plate in one of the display cases that mentioned the Joint.[57] It turned out that in 1948, the plate had been cast by Jews at the JDC-supported Föhrenwald Displaced Persons Camp near Munich, Germany. Instead of the traditional Hebrew phrase

---

[57] A seder plate displays ritual foods that are part of a Passover seder.

le-shanah ha-ba-a b'Yerushalayim, "next year in Jerusalem," the Föhrenwald plate read *be-shanah ha-zot b'Yerushalayim,* "this year in Jerusalem."[58] Three weeks after that seder attended by Holocaust survivors, the State of Israel came into existence.

Ted Comet of JDC arranged for the plate to be reproduced as a special numbered series. Two hundred were cast to be given to new members of the Warburg Society at their annual dinner. Now, Kolker and a half-dozen other carefully selected board members began to solicit the other members of the board.

The Board's New Resource Development Committee

Soliciting JDC board members for donations would raise some money, but the board had even more to offer by helping the new resource development program identify potential donors outside of JDC and open doors to them. Art Sandler, a real estate developer who joined the JDC board in 1995, was appointed the first chair of the new board committee created for this purpose.

Since JDC did not have a fundraising department, there was a great deal of initial work involved in starting one. Goals and objectives had to be established, and fundraisers and support staff needed to be hired. Marketing materials had to be developed and designed. The new board committee closely followed Kolker's blueprint and worked with Alan Gill in Israel. Sandler recalls the complications involved in working with Gill: "It was a little cumbersome. He was in Israel. The action was happening here."[59] Early fundraising efforts focused on Holocaust survivors and a few dozen wealthy federation donors who were oriented toward JDC's work.

Tensions soon began to arise over the ground rules for solicitations that Kolker and Schneider had developed. Some JDC staff and board wanted to pursue donors more aggressively. Sandler recalls the discussions:

---

[58] For a photo of the Föhrenwald plate, see http://typo3.ort.org/index.php?id=224.

[59] Art Sandler, interview, March 7, 2007.

There were some people who wanted to say, look, just tell the federations we're going to go raise money, that's all. Let the chips fall where they may. And there were others who said, no, no...we can't do that. We have to be respectful. They're our biggest donor and we have to do things with them or around them and not interfere, not hurt them. Nobody wanted to hurt them, but we wanted to be a little more aggressive... some of us wanted to do it quicker, bigger, faster, but JDC had its way and was viewed respectfully.

Despite JDC's elaborate planning process, carefully designed ground rules, motivated board committee, and acute need for funding, the new resource development program started out slowly. It was not easy to identify new donors who were willing to give a minimum of $250,000, and establishing donor-sensitivity among JDC staff was a challenge.

Chapter 5: New Relationships with Federations and the Federation System

The Rescue of Ethiopian Jews

Throughout its history, JDC periodically faced situations that required rescuing Jews in danger. As a result, JDC developed considerable experience in planning and executing these rescues, which needed to be conducted in total secrecy so as not to jeopardize lives. The stories of JDC's successful rescue operations of Jews in Yemen, Syria, Iran, and Yugoslavia remain largely untold as JDC has always tended to understate its achievements. However, one such rescue story, involving Ethiopian Jews, is now public knowledge.

Ethiopian Jews claim that even before the beginning of the Common Era, they had their own community in rural Ethiopia. Calling themselves the *Beta Israel*, their tradition maintains that throughout the centuries, they continually practiced a version of Judaism that pre-dated the Talmudic era, enduring the vicissitudes of Ethiopian history and remaining largely isolated from world Jewry.

Their situation, never comfortable, began to deteriorate in 1973, when Colonel Mengistu Haile Mariam replaced Emperor Haile Selassie following a Marxist-Leninist coup. Under Mengistu's dictatorship, Judaism and the teaching of Hebrew were banned.

The Israeli government, under the leadership of Prime

Minister Menachem Begin, initiated attempts to bring oppressed Ethiopian Jews to Israel. In 1984, over the course of six weeks, almost 8,000 were successfully rescued after they walked on foot for weeks to neighboring Sudan during what became known as Operation Moses. An estimated 4,000 perished during the arduous trek. The rescue operation came to an unfortunate end when news leaks alerted Arab nations, which then put strong pressure on the Sudan government to curtail its involvement. Almost 15,000 Jews were left behind, and Mengistu refused to let any more leave.

Seven years later, the Israeli government, represented by Uri Lubrani, began to engage in secret talks with Mengistu and his Hebrew-speaking advisor Kassa Kebede as the regime began to weaken under pressure from rebel factions.[60] Ethiopian Jews would be in mortal danger if the rebels succeeded in their efforts to topple the government. Mengistu and Kebede indicated a willingness to release the remaining Jews in exchange for $35 million, a ransom figure arrived at only after tough negotiations.

To plan the rescue operation, the Israeli government began to work with a representative of the American government and Michael Schneider of JDC. The Bush administration would provide diplomatic and financial support, while JDC would contribute its rescue expertise, especially valuable since JDC had already become involved with Ethiopian Jewry. The Bush administration, represented by Senator Rudy Boschwitz of Minnesota, agreed to allocate $15 million to pay for an emergency airlift. The ransom money, however, would have to come from elsewhere.

Paying money for the release of Jews was not unprecedented for JDC. An emergency endowment fund had been in existence for many years largely for this very purpose. However, in this particular circumstance, the amount requested was far beyond the funding principles that JDC had established. While JDC did have the money to ransom these Jews, it elected to

---

[60] For details of the talks and subsequent rescue operation, see Spector, 2004.

approach the federation system for the money so as not to deplete its reserves.

Michael Schneider recognized that the Jewish Agency for Israel needed to be involved, since the organization would be required to play a part in the transfer of any funds and would be responsible for the Ethiopians once they arrived in Israel. At an emergency meeting in New York arranged by Schneider, leaders from CJF, UJA, and JAFI agreed to the $35 million ransom payment. The amount would be drawn from funds that had already been collected by federations and designated for overseas needs.

In May 1991, as the operation was being planned, Mengistu fled the country for sanctuary in Zimbabwe. Kebede remained, hoping for sanctuary in Israel. Rebels headed toward the Ethiopian capital, Addis Ababa, where the Jews were situated. It was imperative that the rescue begin as soon as possible.

Operation Solomon commenced on Friday, May 24, 1991. A total of 34 commercial and military jets, with their seats removed to maximize capacity, transported 14,310 Ethiopian Jews to Israel over the course of 34 hours. The Israeli airline, El Al, received special rabbinic permission to operate on the Jewish Sabbath, since lives were at stake. The median age of the Ethiopians rescued was under 15.

All of Israel and world Jewry rejoiced once the intricately planned operation became public knowledge. Uri Lubrani, the Jewish Agency for Israel, and the Israeli Defense Forces received the credit for its spectacular success. JDC was barely acknowledged. The $35 million ransom became the property of the new Ethiopian government.

The State of Israel now had the responsibility of assisting these new immigrants and integrating them into Israeli society. JDC-Israel would play a role in this regard. It would be a challenge unlike any the country had previously encountered with other immigrant populations.

A Radical Move by the Cleveland Federation

Although federations were increasingly giving small sums of money directly to overseas agencies, bypassing UJA, the first federation to really break rank in a significant way was Cleveland. Cleveland raised about $26 million each year and split the money 60/40 between local needs and overseas needs, giving between $10 and $11 million annually to UJA.

In 1997, Stephen Hoffman, the federation executive in Cleveland, working with the federation's lay board, started a new initiative called Overseas Connections, which had been strongly recommended in the federation's recently issued strategic planning document. The initiative called for $3 million to be pulled from the yearly allocation to the United Jewish Appeal. This money would instead be designated through a lay committee process for specific overseas programs. Given Cleveland's conservative, Midwest mindset, this was a radical move.

Overseas Connections was driven by two considerations. First, Cleveland, like other federations, was unhappy with JAFI, finding it inefficient, unresponsive to the concerns of North American Jewry, and lacking transparency. Taking money out of the overseas funding system would send JAFI a clear message and, it was hoped, motivate change. Second, the new initiative was an attempt to create personal bonds between donors and specific overseas projects. The current system that provided donors with only generalized understandings of the activities of JAFI and JDC created little emotional connection. Cleveland donors were not excited enough about donating to overseas Jewry since they had little or no understanding of where their money was going or who was benefiting from it. At best, during a mission to Israel, they might ride a bus past a building, hear someone mention that the Cleveland federation had provided partial support for the building, feel proud, and keep going. Donors wanted to follow their money.

Cleveland's problem was with UJA and JAFI, so the federation did not want to penalize JDC when it removed $3 million from the overseas funding system. It decided to set aside $690,000, representing the amount JDC would have received from the existing UJA split formula, and send it directly to JDC. That left about $2.3 million for other programs.

S. Lee Kohrman, a Cleveland attorney who chaired the Overseas Connections committee and later joined the JDC board, describes the criteria that the lay committee planned to use in determining how to spend the money:

> *We wanted to spend our money wisely using various criteria...that we could have a real impact, that our money could be reasonably transformational and we could spend it in large pieces, that the money we would be giving would be welcomed by a service organization to help deal with something they felt passionate about that was very high on their list of priorities, that the program would have a high likelihood of inspiring Clevelanders to participate.[61]*

The committee was in agreement that they wanted to help Ethiopian immigrants. It was now six years since Operation Solomon, and there had been a number of accounts in the American Jewish press about the difficulties these immigrants were experiencing in their efforts to become integrated into Israeli society. Federation money had brought them to Israel, and federations felt an obligation to help them integrate into Israeli society.

On a subsequent trip to Israel, Hoffman arranged a meeting with Alan Gill at JDC-Israel offices. The two were longtime friends, as Gill grew up in Cleveland and served as the federation executive in nearby Columbus. Gill recalls the conversation:

> *Steve Hoffman...walked into my office...and he said 'I'm not sleeping at night over the Ethiopians in Israel. What would a million dollars do?' I said 'where in the*

---

[61] S. Lee Kohrman, interview, February 19, 2007.

hell are you going to get a million dollars a year?' He said 'that's my problem, not yours'....I said 'you're serious?' And he said 'yes.' Now little did I know they were in the process of taking $3 million out of their campaign and they were going to designate a million just for the Ethiopian-Israelis and it was up for grabs between us, the [Jewish] Agency, and very possibly other organizations.

Gill walked Hoffman over to the JDC-Brookdale Institute, and discussed this opportunity with Jack Habib, who agreed to prepare a broad overview of the state of Ethiopian-Israeli absorption and the myriad of interventions, public and private non-profit, that were in operation at that time.

Cleveland ended up receiving a detailed list of about 25 possible program options. One item on the list caught the committee's attention – a currently unfunded proposal to increase the number of young Ethiopian children attending preschool.

Following the mass arrival of the Ethiopians in 1991, the Israeli government, with help from JDC-Israel, developed a full array of social programs for them. However, according to JDC-Brookdale research, very young children were not being served. Compared with any other immigrant group, only a small percentage of these children were attending preschools. Ethiopian parents could not afford to enroll their children, and even when they could, sending children away from home at a young age to be cared for by someone else was not part of their culture.

The result was that children of Ethiopian immigrants were developmentally far behind their Israeli peers. Without the valuable skills and experiences acquired in preschool, Ethiopian children were struggling from the moment they enrolled in Israeli schools. Ethiopian parents were mostly illiterate, spoke their native Amharic language at home, and did not provide much educational stimulation. This approach may have been appropriate for their former rural agrarian society but was problematic for a successful life in modern Israel. Early childhood research is unequivocal that the first few years of life are critical for language acquisition and brain development. Israel needed the equivalent of a Head Start program for Ethiopians.

Cleveland's Overseas Connections committee then asked the JDC-Brookdale Institute for additional information about the proposed preschool program. JDC-Brookdale provided an extensive, customized response, and the committee began to consider the program seriously. From their perspective, the gap between the Ethiopians and other groups of children with respect to readiness for school was so large that it would be a relatively straightforward process to study whether special preschool programs for Ethiopian children were effective in closing it. Such a study would meet one of the committee's criteria – that any program chosen have a significant and measurable impact.

The $1 million that Cleveland was interested in investing would fund a program that was considerably larger in scope than anything JDC-Israel was accustomed to implementing. Typically, pilot projects conceived by JDC-Israel were not large-scale programs. Cleveland was interested in piloting a program that would affect as many as 800 Ethiopian children ages six and under. The city of Beersheva, located in the Negev desert, was selected as the site, since it had a large Ethiopian population, and JDC already had a strong presence and good working relationships there.

JDC and the Overseas Connection committee went back and forth a number of times to finalize the project proposal. The process was new to both sides, since no federation had ever been involved in the design of a JDC program. The collaboration did not always go smoothly.

At a key meeting in Israel, Cleveland's Overseas Connections committee brought in a national expert on Head Start programs, Arthur Naparstek, a professor of social work at Case Western Reserve University in Cleveland.[62] Naparstek,

---

[62] Naparstek died in April 2004. The narrative presented here is based on Alan Gill's recollections.

after reviewing the proposal, spotted a significant shortcoming in the program's design. The program was focused exclusively on children and did not include the home environment or the school setting. Research had consistently demonstrated that for school readiness programs to be successful, the child's home environment and the educational system needed attention, not just the child.

Naparstek was not perceived as being very tactful in presenting his professional opinion to JDC at the meeting. Despite Alan Gill's efforts to keep things calm, sparks flew. JDC was completely unused to working with funders in this fashion, and had, throughout its history, operated with a certain degree of self-assuredness regarding its expertise in program development. Funders provided money, while JDC managed the relationship and maintained sole ownership of programs, with no input from donors. Yet here was an outside party challenging JDC's program expertise, and more fundamentally, the nature of the relationship between funder and JDC. Cleveland was not content to write a check and let JDC do the work – it wanted to be a partner in the program's creation and design.

JDC, to its credit, was willing to examine Naparstek's critique objectively. JDC eventually recognized that the argument had considerable merit, and JDC staff member Rami Sulimani revised the program's design based on Cleveland's input. This adaptation led to the choice of a name for the program – PACT, an acronym for Parents and Children Together. PACT would not just be a preschool program – it would also include baby clinics, daycare for children too young for preschool, and home interventions with parents.

JDC had enacted its first true partnership with a federation.

Managing the New Partnership with Cleveland

Once PACT was up and running, the Cleveland federation could, for the first time, showcase a specific overseas program to contributors, providing them with an opportunity to see exactly how their money was being spent. Donors from Cleveland who visited Israel on a mission were no longer limited to driving past a federation-funded building on a bus tour. They could now get off the bus, enter a Beersheva preschool or visit a health clinic, and meet Ethiopian children. Mission-goers could view Ethiopian children's artwork, play a game with them, watch them engage in Israeli dancing, and hear them sing. Very quickly, every single mission coming to Israel from Cleveland went to Beersheva – donors, lay leaders, teen groups, even Cleveland civic officials who were not Jewish.

These missions made significant demands on JDC's new resource development department, demands that JDC did not anticipate when the department was established. Alan Gill's group now had responsibility for orchestrating the logistics for these missions, organizing the schedule and attending to every minor detail. Many mundane questions arose. Who picked up at the airport? Were the buses and restrooms clean? Were the bus drivers willing to refrain from smoking? Who printed and hung the welcome banner? Was there a decent kosher restaurant in the vicinity? Which classrooms were visited? Which preschool teachers and school administrators in Beersheva were the most fluent in English?

Eliot Goldstein, who managed PACT relationships and mission logistics when the program was first launched, summarizes his job description:

> *I'm the cultural mediator, I'm the literal and figurative translator, I'm the mission manager, I'm the sales person, I'm the customer relations guy, I'm the ego massager, I'm the time manager, I'm the maschgiach[63] for kosher food.[64]*

---

[63] A Hebrew term describing someone who supervises the kosher procedures of a food establishment.

[64] Eliot Goldstein, interview, April 28, 2006.

Apart from mission logistics, the partnership placed a number of other new demands on JDC's resource development department. Cleveland's Overseas Connections committee requested data describing PACT program results to see if the program was accomplishing its goals. This effort required the involvement of the JDC-Brookdale Institute. JDC also needed to design brochures and literature to serve as marketing materials that could be distributed to donors. Video conference calls and visits to Cleveland by JDC staff began to take place regularly in order to explain the program, inspire donors, maintain the program's visibility, and discuss how it was evolving. Memos needed to be written about strategic issues and donor cultivation.

JDC's resource development department, which had started out slowly with a focus on an elite group of wealthy individual donors, now grew quickly to meet the demands of this unanticipated federation partnership.

Gideon Herscher, former director of Ethiopian and Israeli Partnerships at JDC, describes the overall impact of the program on federations: "[PACT]…was exactly what American Jewry, specifically federation donors, needed at that time. And not only federation donors but the federations themselves as a professional fundraising body…we were a fantastic fundraising tool."[65]

For the first time, PACT enabled federation donors to follow their dollars. PACT, in comparison with other JDC programs, was especially attractive to federation donors because it evoked such primal human values. All parents want their children to succeed. The possibility that without intervention an entire people would grow up to become an underclass touched the donors. There was something they could do to change the future of these Ethiopian children. Furthermore, their federation had helped bring these children to Israel, and donors felt a sense of responsibility to them.[66]

---

[65] Gideon Herscher, interview, May 16, 2006.

[66] In 2008, PACT programs were operating in 14 Israeli cities, with 12,000 children enrolled, representing two out of every three Ethiopian children eligible for PACT. Of the $21 million budget, 61% is provided

Cleveland's decision to break from the national funding system foreshadowed change at a national level in the federation system. Shortly, the entire overseas funding system would undergo a major reorganization, generating further demands on JDC's resource development department and requiring JDC field staff to operate with a fundraising mentality.

The Creation of the United Jewish Communities

The federation group that had started to analyze the national funding system in 1993 began a prolonged and complex negotiation and study process that culminated six years later in the creation of a new entity, the United Jewish Communities.[67] The major players in the negotiations were the Council of Jewish Federations, which was owned by the federations, the United Jewish Appeal, which was co-owned by JDC, and the United Israel Appeal. Press accounts and public statements described the process as a merger, but the reality was otherwise. What in fact transpired was a takeover by the system of federations seeking ownership of the entire funding system.

While many issues were debated and discussed during the negotiations, concerns by the federations about allocations to overseas Jewry were central and pervasive, "one of the driving forces behind the creation of the UJC," according to one press account.[68] Although the federations did the fundraising for the national system, the existing structure gave them little or no say in how money was allocated overseas, or who received it. The federations argued that since they raised the money, they

---

by municipalities and the Israeli government, and 39% is provided by federations, foundations, and individual donors.

[67] For more detail about the creation of the United Jewish Communities, see Jeffrey R. Solomon and Susan H. Wachsstock, "Reflections on the UJC Merger: Issues Faced and Lessons Learned." *Journal of Jewish Communal Service,* Fall 2002; Bubis and Windmuller, 2005.

[68] Julia Goldman, "Focus on Issues: Federations Begin to Re-Examine Process of Funding Needs Abroad." *Jewish Telegraphic Agency,* August 18, 1999.

should determine how it was to be spent. One of the reasons that the negotiation process was so lengthy was because the issue was so contentious.

Although the transition was not a hostile takeover – UJA and UIA ultimately agreed to become part of the new organization – they did so with a considerable degree of reluctance. Their primary concern was that overseas allocations would continue to decline in the absence of their advocacy. At several points during the negotiations, UJA attempted to institute an agreement whereby each federation would be required to allocate a minimum amount for overseas needs. The federations were strongly opposed to any such requirement, and the issue became a deal breaker. Ultimately, it was never instituted in the final agreement.

The concerns of UJA and UIA were counterbalanced by the reality of the numbers. Revenues for overseas Jewry had continued to decline over the past decade (see Table A3 in Appendix A). The falling revenues forced UJA and UIA to acknowledge that their advocacy had not been able to reverse the decline. Perhaps, the negotiators reasoned among themselves, the needs of overseas Jewry could attain new visibility among donors if federations were to own the system. With the right approaches, the United Jewish Communities might be able to enliven an area that was no longer attracting donor interest.

The creation of the new system provided JDC with a promising opportunity. For the previous sixty-five years, starting with the establishment of the United Jewish Appeal in 1934, JDC and UIA regularly clashed over how to split the money raised for overseas Jewry. With the demise of UJA, a new procedure would have to be established. Michael Schneider had been pushing for such a change ever since his frustrating attempts in 1989 to obtain additional funding for JDC when Soviet Jews were stranded in Ladispoli.

JDC wanted any new allocation method to give greater consideration to needs in the field, since the Zionist ideology of the Jewish Agency for Israel had, for many years, been the prevailing influence over the allocation of funds. JAFI had continued to receive roughly $3 for every $1 that JDC received largely because UJA, as the intermediary between federations and JAFI, had served as a buffer against federation dissatisfaction with JAFI. Without UJA, and with federations making decisions based on realities in the field, the current 75/25 split might shift more in JDC's favor, or so JDC hoped.

A New Method for Distributing Money Overseas[69]

Michael Schneider presented JDC's position early in the negotiations. JDC would support whatever arrangement CJF, UJA, and UIA agreed upon, as long as it included a new process for distributing overseas allocations that was independent, non-political, and controlled by the federations. Schneider believed that JDC could only benefit if funding decisions were under federation control, especially given recent efforts by Alan Gill and his team to strengthen federation relations.

Schneider, in close consultation with JDC board president Jonathan Kolker and other JDC staff, took the initiative and formulated guidelines for a proposed needs-based system, which would be created by the newly-formed Overseas Needs Assessment and Distributions (ONAD) committee at UJC. Their plan was discussed at a series of meetings and distributed to the leaders of the forty largest federations. Kolker chaired the ensuing planning committee, working closely with Steve Nasatir, the federation executive from Chicago. Kolker, like Schneider, believed strongly that "funds [should] follow needs instead of historic formulas," and hoped that he could help craft a new funding mechanism.

One of the few influential individuals who withheld support for the proposed plan was Charles Goodman, the chair of the Board of Governors of JAFI. He felt the plan did not focus on the real problem, which he viewed as the erosion of the collective responsibility model for overseas funding and the ascendance of decision-making by individual federations. Goodman's position, however, represented a small minority.

---

[69] This history of the Overseas Needs Assessment and Distributions Committee draws from Hessel, 2007c and Kolker, 2005.

While there was a handful of federation executives who shared his philosophy and felt strongly that the collective system needed to be preserved, the dominant perspective acknowledged and accepted current philanthropic trends. It was futile to try to convince a new generation of donors to give to an abstract collective system. They had little interest in putting their money into a "black box."

Kolker's involvement resulted in a final plan that closely resembled the initial JDC proposal. The ONAD committee was to consist of 25 members – 18 members from federations, 3 from JDC, 3 from JAFI, and a committee chair. Each federation on the committee would be represented by the executive and board chair, which would ensure that all voices in the federation would be heard.

Determining which federations would have representation on the committee was not a simple matter. Some federations gave far more to overseas Jewry than others, and consequently expected a commensurate role on the committee. Certain federations were more favorably inclined toward JDC than JAFI. Others had major donors who were members of the JAFI board and would forcefully argue for the JAFI position in allocation discussions. What resulted was a complex arrangement in which membership on the committee rotated by lottery among federations based on their size, with New York and Chicago, the two federations with the largest overseas allocations, assigned permanent seats.

The first ONAD chair, Alan Jaffe, was asked to serve by philanthropist Charles Bronfman, who became the first board chair of the new United Jewish Communities. Jaffe, who at the time was managing partner of a Manhattan law firm, had the requisite credentials. He had served as the lay president of the New York federation, was on the JDC board, was a member of the Board of Governors of JAFI, and had been an officer of the Council of Jewish Federations. Jaffe was also extensively involved in the negotiations to form UJC.

Now that the Jewish Agency for Israel held three seats on the committee, they would no longer be dealing with the federation system through an intermediary. JAFI would be sitting at the table with federation executives, and federation executives would have input into the Jewish Agency's programs and budget. This new system was just what the federations had been wanting. No such arrangement had ever existed, going back all the way to the creation of the Jewish Agency for Palestine in the 1920s.

The first meeting of the ONAD committee was held in August 1999. The members agreed to conduct a global needs assessment, and representatives visited communities in Israel and the former Soviet Union served by JAFI and JDC programs. However, the ONAD committee subsequently decided to postpone this assessment, recognizing that the task was too vast and would not readily lend itself to specific allocation decisions. What the committee focused on instead was making a distinction between "core" needs, to which all federations would contribute, and "elective" needs, which would be discretionary.

Within a year, the ONAD committee decided that 90 percent of the money raised by each federation for overseas Jewry would be considered core funding, and would be sent to the United Jewish Communities as the successor of the United Jewish Appeal. The remaining 10 percent of overseas money, now known as elective funding, could be allocated in whatever fashion a federation wished. This money would go directly to programs and agencies chosen by the federation. Unlike the past, when for all practical purposes all overseas money went to either UIA or JDC, this new approach left the door open for certain other agencies as well.

In essence, the ONAD committee had institutionalized what had already been taking place – the inclination on the part of more and more federations to pull money from the collective system and give it to specific programs in order to inspire donors. Cleveland's decision to remove $3 million was only the most dramatic instance. Henceforth, federations could designate money for specific programs as an officially sanctioned part of the funding system.

Important questions still needed to be answered. First, which programs would fall under the core category and which would be elective? There were disagreements among ONAD representatives, particularly from the Boston federation. Second, how should the core money be split? Should the existing 75/25 split between JDC and JAFI remain intact or change to more accurately reflect overseas needs?

The ONAD committee eventually decided to maintain the existing split formula so as not to "destabilize the existing funding mechanisms," in the words of chair Alan Jaffe.[70] Stephen Hoffman, chief professional officer for the Jewish Federation of Cleveland, who also served as chief executive officer and president of UJC, recalls the deliberations that took place to decide whether the split formula should change or stay the same:

> *Going into the process the first time the conventional betting was that the JDC would wow everybody, the Jewish Agency would stumble in making its case and the money allocations would shift...but it didn't turn out that way. The Jewish Agency made a very compelling case, and the JDC kind of made a blasé effort, which shocked everybody...the Jewish Agency really worked at it and explained everything and at the end of the day the committee voted to keep it where it was, 75/25.[71]*

Even though the split formula remained intact, with the creation of the elective funding, JAFI and JDC entered new territory. UJA had always done the advocacy on JAFI and JDC's behalf. Now, they would need to do their own "marketing" directly to individual federations. The elective money was up for grabs, and each would need to convince federations that their programs were the more deserving ones.

JAFI, in the face of declining immigration to Israel, recast

---

[70] Alan Jaffe, interview, February 13, 2007.

[71] Stephen Hoffman, interview, July 25, 2007

its mission beyond aliyah to include Jewish-Zionist education and partnerships with Israel, positioning itself to preserve its 75 percent share of the elective money. Jeff Kaye, director of Resource Development and Public Affairs for the Jewish Agency for Israel, saw the merger and emergence of the ONAD process as a highly positive development:

> *The merger was actually the best thing that ever happened to us because it forced us to create core capacities that we never had, including talking to donors, being responsive, evaluating, raising [money]. It wouldn't have happened under the old model.*[72]

JDC saw the development as an opportunity to increase its share beyond the 25 percent it had been receiving. The tensions between the two agencies over funding took on a new character. A conflict that had been confined to a series of sessions every few years involving two small groups of JDC and JAFI representatives now played out in every federation in the United States on an ongoing basis.

JDC began to replicate the Cleveland partnership model with other federations around the country. To maintain the same funding from federations required a convincing case. New strategies were needed in order to sustain JDC's share of the 10 percent set aside for elective funding that had previously been core money.

Increasing Market Share

In the summer of 1999, Michael Novick, the federation executive for Seattle, received a phone call from Alan Gill. Gill was making calls to his friends and former federation colleagues to see if they could help him identify a potential candidate for a new position that JDC was creating, that of resource development officer, which would be principally focused on JDC's relations with major federations.

---

[72] Jeff Kaye, interview, August 13, 2008.

Novick, who spent the summer of 1997 on a sabbatical in Israel with JDC, was immediately interested in the position but unwilling to uproot his family and move to New York. After some discussion, he accepted the position and became the first JDC senior staff member not based in New York or Israel. He maintained a home office in Seattle.

However, before he began the position, it turned into something else. The ONAD committee had just been formed, and JDC wanted Novick to serve as an "account manager" who would oversee JDC's individual relationships with federations and work with them to influence the new ONAD-based elective funding decisions in favor of JDC. Up to this point, Gill and his team were responsible for relationships with federations, but under the new funding arrangement the responsibilities would be too demanding. The idea was for Novick to assume most of the relationships over time. He immediately began traveling to federations, explaining JDC's work:

> *Our task was to help them identify some special part of the world where we were already responding to needs, but that they could attach their name to...if they had an interest in exploring other parts of the world, the former Soviet Union, Romania, Bulgaria, whatever it might be, we would try to help develop that partnership, that linkage.*[73]

The hope was that by providing federations with opportunities to connect donors to specific programs, much as Cleveland had connected donors with Ethiopian families in Israel, JDC would continue to receive at least the 25 percent it would have been allocated under the old arrangement. With skill and diligence, it might increase the share beyond 25 percent, or even secure additional funding.

Simultaneously, the Jewish Agency for Israel devised a similar approach, appointing David Sarnat, the former federation executive from Atlanta, to travel the same circuit as

---

[73] Michael Novick, interview, February 26, 2007.

Novick. The two often presented in tandem. Each made the case as to why the elective funding should go to his organization and his projects.

What Novick and Sarnat encountered during most of their initial visits were federations that did not yet have a process to make informed decisions about the new elective funding they were now empowered to spend. The Cleveland federation's Overseas Connections committee was ahead of its time. Novick describes the situation he faced:

> *For the most part, when the ONAD process began, most federations did not have active Israel and overseas committees to make decisions on how the 10 percent was supposed to be split and what projects or what needs they wanted to target their dollars for. What quickly emerged in that first year was the federations started appointing these committees.*

Even after Israel and overseas committees began to form, Novick realized that federations still needed educating. When federation executives, staff, and lay leaders went on missions, they almost always went to Israel. Novick noted that few knew about JDC's work in other countries: "It became very clear to me that most involved leaders, including staff of federations, didn't have a clue about the length and breadth and scope of JDC's reach."

Novick developed PowerPoint visuals that provided federations with information about JDC programs and data regarding how federation money was being used. The idea was to bring the field to the donor. These presentations were initially effective, but over time federations wanted more information than Novick alone could provide. To maintain their interest and involvement, Novick expanded the concept of bringing the field to the donor by inviting articulate and knowledgeable field staff to speak at federations, a practice that came to be known within JDC as "outbound." JDC "stars," inspiring speakers with fluent English, from such cities as Budapest, Kiev, or

Buenos Aires, traveled around the United States telling their stories to federation donors. This approach strengthened JDC-federation relationships and created a real sense of excitement among donors. Sometimes, it led to federation missions to these countries, cementing the relationship. These new relationships with federations required an enormous amount of work. Eliot Goldstein describes the emerging requirements for JDC:

> *[Federations] need proposals. They need budgets. If they approve [the proposal] they then need mission visits and pictures and plaques and photos and stories and banners and banquets....We have to work much harder to earn back the money we used to get for free....Instead of getting one check for $50 million dollars from the UJA, we are getting quarterly payments from 100 federations for 600 different projects in different amounts going to 60 countries around the world...so this gets very complicated.*

When JDC began to pursue the elective funding, in the words of Michael Schneider, "that is when Gill and company took off big time." As JDC expanded these relationships with federations, the ONAD committee struggled to generate an allocations mechanism that was acceptable to all parties. This effort ultimately proved unsuccessful.

The Failure of ONAD

When the United Jewish Appeal came to an end, so did its advocacy efforts for overseas Jewry. Although UJC and the Overseas Needs Assessment and Distribution committee were able to reduce the rate of decline in overseas allocations from federations that had been taking place before the creation of UJC, they were unable to stop the reduction entirely (see Table A3 in Appendix A).

The primary problem was the voluntary nature of the system. Since each federation made its own decisions regarding the percentages it chose to allocate overseas, there was considerable variation. Percentages of annual campaign revenues sent overseas ranged across federations from a low of 17 percent to a high of 43 percent. UJA had tried to establish a minimum contribution for federations during the negotiations leading to the creation of UJC but was unable to prevail.

ONAD had also been created with an assumption that overseas allocations would increase, not decrease. The decline made it all the more difficult for JDC and JAFI, since they were now being forced to compete for a shrinking amount of core dollars. Doron Krakow, former UJC senior vice-president for Israel and Overseas Needs, recalls the dynamic: "Both the Joint and the Jewish Agency were compelled to make the case as to why they were more worthy on a relative basis than the other, a problem that wouldn't exist if we were in an age of plenty."[74]

The essential issue was whether the long-standing 75/25 split formula between JDC and JAFI would remain the same or shift as a result of the ONAD process. Krakow describes UJC's role:

> *Would the ONAD process have the fortitude to make a change in the status quo ante, and therefore leave its mark from the standpoint of federation leadership... or wouldn't it, as a result of inertia that's born of the politics of the federation leadership's engagement with our overseas partners?*

ONAD was clearly created with a noble intent – to allocate resources in a fashion that would provide the greatest amount of assistance to international Jewry – but this objective was ultimately thwarted by a combination of economics and politics. The same sorts of JDC-JAFI resource battles that had been taking place since the 1930s continued to take place on the ONAD committee, 70 years later.

In 2001, Robert Goldberg, a prominent lay leader from Cleveland who had served as a member of the Board of

---

[74] Doron Krakow, interview, August 1, 2007.

Governors of the Jewish Agency for Israel, was appointed chair following Alan Jaffe, and the ONAD committee entered a new phase. The committee decided to reconsider the 75/25 split formula but postponed the decision a year while federation working groups conducted needs assessments. ONAD also decided to begin an advocacy group to replace the work that was previously performed by the United Jewish Appeal.

In the meantime, JDC faced a budget shortfall of almost $20 million. The economy in Argentina had collapsed, the formerly thriving Jewish community there was economically devastated, and JDC was providing substantial aid. JDC was also continuing to provide support to elderly Jews in the former Soviet Union.

To deal with the budget crisis, JDC sent a letter to federations in February 2003 containing an urgent appeal for them to increase their overseas allocations to JDC through UJC. In writing the letter, JDC bypassed the ONAD committee, and UJC reacted disapprovingly. It promptly sent a letter to JDC complaining about their decision to act unilaterally without consulting UJC, effectively circumventing ONAD.[75] What was not apparent was how this incident was any different from past situations in which JDC had also appealed directly to federations.

Steven Klinghoffer, a past president of the United Jewish Communities of Metrowest New Jersey, assumed the chairmanship of ONAD in 2003. That fall, the ONAD working group responsible for examining social welfare outside of Israel called for a $13 million increase in core funding to JDC, indicating that the money was badly needed for Jews in Argentina and the former Soviet Union. Where would the additional $13 million for JDC come from? Since allocations for overseas needs were not increasing, the additional money would of necessity require a reduction in the Jewish Agency's allocation and a change in the split formula.

The Jewish Agency immediately mobilized to keep this

---

[75] Nacha Cattan, "UJC May Shrink Jewish Agency Funding." *Forward,* November 7, 2003.

shift from happening. They challenged the figures that JDC presented regarding the number of aid recipients in the former Soviet Union and argued forcefully that the Jewish Agency needed the money to respond to terrorism and meet the needs of immigrants in a struggling Israeli economy. Sallai Meridor, the chairman of the Jewish Agency, played his strongest hand to influence the federation representatives.[76] At the General Assembly in Israel that November, he brought in Israel's Prime Minister, Ariel Sharon, to address the ONAD committee. Sharon told the committee members, "You are my guests, so I am asking you to make Israel your number one priority for funding. If you weren't my guests, I would demand it."[77]

While the federation executives did not appreciate Meridor's heavy-handed tactics, they had the desired effect. At the subsequent ONAD meeting in December 2003, under intense pressure from supporters of the Jewish Agency associated with certain key federations, the committee voted to maintain the existing 75/25 split formula and rejected the recommendation of ONAD's working group. To address the legitimate needs of both JDC and JAFI, the federations optimistically agreed to raise an additional $20 million that would be split 50/50. Doron Krakow offers a perspective on what happened:

> There was a JDC camp, a Jewish Agency camp, and their relative power centers within the key federations ... New York ... Chicago ... Detroit ... Cleveland...Baltimore...the system desperately wanted the ONAD process to stake out new ground by asserting some sort of a leadership/ownership role, but the politics resisted that greatly, and in this instance the Jewish Agency, which had the most to gain or to lose, I think, in the collective use of our dollars, because they get three out of every four collective dollars, they

---

[76] In 2006, Meridor was appointed by Israeli Prime Minister Ehud Olmert as the Israeli ambassador to the United States.

[77] Rachel Pomerance, "Israel's Prime Minister Weighs In as Federations Decide on Funding." *Jewish Telegraphic Agency*, November 19, 2003.

wielded their political might seemingly very effectively,
and were able to prevent there being any change in the
collective use of [UJC] dollars.

Alan Jaffe described the vote as the beginning of the end
of the ONAD process:

> *Certain federations were not prepared to alter*
> *the nature of the allocation notwithstanding the*
> *recommendations of ONAD's own committee that*
> *it should be altered....That caused a great crisis in*
> *confidence around the [federation] system about*
> *ONAD, and it effectively was the death knell of*
> *ONAD...ONAD couldn't do its job, couldn't really*
> *make the tough decisions.*

Stephen Hoffman reflects on the nature of a decision process
that involved 25 decision-makers with predetermined biases:
"When you have [this kind of] situation it literally needs to be
overwhelming to get a change...so in the absence of that, the
status quo became the path of consensus."

While the ONAD committee continued to meet after the vote,
federation leaders no longer had confidence in UJC's ability to
impose a new agenda. JDC as well was severely disappointed.
During the negotiations that had led to the creation of UJC,
UJC had agreed to take on the responsibility of reforming
the allocation system so that it was more responsive to needs
around the globe. Despite a considerable investment of time
and resources, UJC failed to bring about these reforms.

Michael Schneider, who retired for health reasons in 2002
in the midst of the ONAD process, reflects on the outcome of
the process he advocated:

> *[The federations] had no idea what they were getting*
> *into, no idea. Having to decide to allocate between*
> *two very tough-minded organizations, both with*

*pretty legitimate needs was going to be a hell of a job,
and I don't think anyone quite realized how difficult.*

Following the vote, JDC and JAFI decided that UJC was only getting in the way and that they would need to work out a deal among themselves. As a result, the two agencies began to meet and explore options without UJC involvement.

Meanwhile, a UJC committee undertook a review of the ONAD process, releasing a report in October 2005.[78] The report called for UJC to take a more active role regarding overseas needs and pointed out the problems inherent in a system of voluntary compliance. Emphasizing the importance of annual campaigns and core dollars for both JDC and JAFI, the report made the following observation about the ONAD process:

> *Experience has proven that it is extraordinarily difficult to change the uses of the current collective core through a public decision-making process. Public decision-making processes tend to polarize positions and engender conflict. For a consensus-driven system, polarization and conflict has not led to resolution.*[79]

The report specifically requested that federations providing a "disproportionately small percentage" to the core increase their level of allocations and recommended consequences for federations not in compliance with the overall policy of collective responsibility. Recommending that the ONAD process be suspended, the committee officially approved the process that was already taking place in which JDC and JAFI negotiated their own two-year agreement to determine the distribution of overseas funds.

What happened, quite simply, was that JDC and JAFI reverted to the pre-ONAD "backroom" negotiations in place

---

[78] Morton Plant, ONAD Review Report, http://www.ujc.org/page.aspx?id=106622.

[79] Morton Plant, ONAD Review Report.

when the United Jewish Appeal existed. UJC would no longer play a meaningful role in determining the split.

While the general consensus was that ONAD had failed, there were some who saw a positive aspect to the process. The ONAD committee's decision to create elective funding brought federations into much closer contact with JDC and JAFI and made the agencies far more visible in the federation world. Federations now had regular contact with JDC and JAFI staff and much greater knowledge of their programs. JDC and JAFI, in turn, learned how to market themselves. Jacob Solomon, executive vice-president of the Greater Miami Jewish Federation, observes:

> *Most people view ONAD as having been a pretty big failure. I don't think it was, because it caused both of our overseas agencies to learn how to present themselves in ways that were constructive, whether for fundraising purposes – which in my opinion is not a happy thing, but an inevitable one – or more importantly, for the purpose of demonstrating the impact of their work to federations.*[80]

Todd Stettner, executive vice president and chief executive officer of the Jewish Federation of Greater Kansas City, feels that ONAD gave JDC far more visibility than it had under the United Jewish Appeal: "When the old UJA existed, JAFI was dominant. You hardly ever heard about JDC....What's happened since ONAD is that JDC has come way up in the front, and JAFI now has taken the backseat."[81]

---

[80] Jacob Solomon, interview, July 5, 2007
[81] Todd Stettner, interview, July 11, 2007.

Chapter 6: Shaking Up the Joint – The New Fundraising Culture

Initial Resistance

Alan Gill's efforts to change the culture at JDC met with resistance almost from the moment he started spending time there, even before he became a full-time employee. The seminar that he, Sara Hirschhorn, and Jack Habib organized for federation leaders in Israel during his first year at JDC, when he was executive in residence, placed considerable demands on JDC-Israel staff. In order for the seminar to be successful, he needed staff cooperation. Although JDC-Israel staff did participate, it was with more than a little reluctance. Gill recalls their reactions:

> *We put the program divisions through hell to have that seminar. Why? For some future point when the United Jewish Appeal really goes under, when federations truly start [to give directly to JDC]. There was no money on the table. So we were really resented by field partners....I tried my best...to sell people on it...I was basically telling them, 'Here is the way things are going to be in the future. In order to benefit later, this is what we need you to do now. We are asking you to spend a lot of energy and some of your own internal budget to send staff out to show federation people around while they are in Israel, even though you're not going to see anything from it towards your budget this year.'*

Outside observers did not quite understand what Gill was doing either. As one example, Jack Ukeles, who served as an organizational development consultant to JDC, shares his memories prior to working for the organization:

> *[When JDC started] building relations with federations, it struck me at the time as sort of pointless because it was still the era of the big pot of dough.... But when I look back now, it was an incredible piece of foresight...to gear up over a very long period of time, to the point where there's this incredibly powerful fundraising machine.*[82]

Alan Gill had seen the future, and he was actively working to position JDC to benefit from the anticipated funding shifts, but very few people either within or outside of JDC appreciated his vision. He had the full support of Michael Schneider, but it took time to convince everyone else that what he was asking them to do was necessary and important. Although he was making demands on JDC staff, he could not promise much in return, only a hope that their efforts would eventually generate funding at some unspecified future time, which he sometimes referred to as "money for later." It was a lot to ask.

Rebecca Caspi served as Alan Gill's deputy for JDC's newly formed resource development department during this period.[83] Caspi describes the typical perspective of JDC field professionals during the early years of the new resource development program:

> *Our field partners had no awareness of why [resource development activities were] important. They viewed them as a huge burden....It was a very shocking time. They lived in an environment where they proposed*

---

[82]   Jack Ukeles, interview, March 14, 2007.

[83]   Caspi is currently senior vice-president, Global Operations: Israel and Overseas for the United Jewish Communities.

a program or a series of programs which they had
every intent of doing. They got budget from the Joint
in New York, which was available and mostly covered
their needs...there was much tension around the
perceived to be unreasonable demands [from us] and
a sense of what's the point? I get my budget anyway,
why should I do this?[84]

Gill's team recognized that they needed to work on improving relationships with field professionals just as they built relationships with federations. Missions placed new demands on field professionals. Their cooperation would not be automatic.

Building Internal Relationships

Any change process is facilitated when there is buy-in from influential individuals. However, key staff did not begin to appreciate why the new resource development efforts were important until new funding finally started flowing in to JDC. That did not happen right away, so cooperation came slowly.

Gill's team made a considerable effort to develop a cooperative working relationship with field professionals. Once federation missions started to take off, it was important for the resource development department to acquire an understanding of what field professionals would or would not do with respect to donor engagement. This could be accomplished only by asking the staff about their needs and spending time with them. Rebecca Caspi describes the process:

You get in the trenches with these people, and you
struggle with them, and you talk about what they're
comfortable with and what they're not comfortable
with and what they're going to be able to keep doing
and what they're not....And you never lose sight
of the fact that all of us together are here to serve

---

[84]   Rebecca Caspi, interview, May 14, 2006.

our clients...if you can stay focused on that most everybody at JDC will respect you for it....This is about raising money to serve people who don't have anybody else to serve them the way JDC can do it.... On Alan's team...we pushed things to the limit time and time again. We tried very hard never to go past it. And when a field colleague said 'This is as far as we're going to go,' we accepted that.

While the resource development staff invested time so they could better understand field professionals, the field professionals did not necessarily reciprocate. In general, they tended to have a negative perception of the fundraising profession. The assumption was that fundraising was something anyone could do. They did not appreciate the skills and advance work required to successfully cultivate donors. For example, it might take months of planning for someone in resource development to line up a single lunch with a donor. Furthermore, field professionals did not necessarily realize that there was an effective and an ineffective way to ask a donor for money.

Even though resource development staff were responsible for most aspects of the fundraising process, they still needed to step aside at times to let field professionals do the talking. No matter how prepared fundraisers might be, they could never substitute for field professionals, who had intimate knowledge of a program and were able to describe it with depth and passion.

Field professionals could be effective in this role only if they were fluent in English. Translators just were not as effective when it came to inspiring donors on missions. Because English fluency was now so crucial for donor relations, highly valued JDC employees suddenly found themselves scrambling to learn English. Whereas previously, jobs went to candidates with the best qualifications, under the new fundraising culture, the best candidate did not necessarily get the job if his or her English was not good enough. Rebecca Caspi describes the changes:

We began to influence what the field was looking for in certain positions. They began to understand and even designate staff lines to work with donors or to work with resource development to work with donors. They began to internalize that they needed this effort, and they needed to dedicate resources to it if they were going to garner the funds they needed to continue or grow their programs. For them, that might have meant making sure they had decent English speakers, making sure they had people with some good social skills...in addition to the core business skills that they need to run programs.

Arnon Mantver, Director-General of JDC-Israel, comments on the changes for JDC staff in Israel:

The basic job descriptions of the upper echelons of JDC and JDC in general have changed....It's harder to find the right people....You have to have Israelis that know how to communicate in English and have the skills of managing partnerships internally within JDC, in Israel, and overseas.[85]

The new emphasis on fundraising was hard on JDC staff. Galit Sagie, a staffperson for ELKA, a division of JDC-Israel that provides training and development programs for public sector professionals, describes the challenges she now faces:

It's been a very, very drastic change, and it has not been easy for a lot of professional staff here because the work is very different than what it was when I came in. When I came in the only thing that mattered was to do your job professionally. I would sit for hours and hours discussing the need for the highest quality....Today, we now also think about how much money our programs raise....We have not given up

---

[85] Arnon Mantver, interview, November 9, 2006.

on any of the standards we had before…it has to be professional and it has to be unique and it has to add value to the market and all those things have remained, but it also has to be marketable and you have to be able to raise funds for it, and that is an added piece of pressure that has made it very hard.[86]

Aside from the demands regarding English and the pressures to raise money, field professionals found themselves needing to distill their complex work into a short presentation that sometimes felt like a stage performance. They had an hour at most to describe to donors work that might have been going on for a year or more in a high-stakes setting.

Gill's team gradually earned the respect of these field professionals by being open and candid with them. Whenever possible, field professionals were given advance notice regarding activities involving a donor, and the resource development staff always tried to provide explanations for any requests. The system was not flawless. For example, a donor might call a day in advance because he happened to be in Israel and wanted a tour of the JDC program his donation was supporting. Field professionals would have to rearrange their schedules at the last minute for these donors, or even cancel days off with family if the donor was sufficiently important.

Despite the best efforts of resource development staff, field professionals were sometimes disappointed. In cases where donors were choosing among several programs, JDC would carefully consider program priorities and steer donors toward certain programs. JDC had a policy of selling and promoting programs that were identified as high priority. Field professionals whose program lost out to another program under this policy were disinclined to trust resource development the next time around. Top management needed to get involved to deal with the resulting resentment.

Although efforts to build trust with field professionals were crucial, building trust within the resource development function

---

[86] Galit Sagie, interview, January 15, 2007.

was just as vital. Alan Gill's overriding philosophy was that there could be no individual wins and that everything needed to be a team effort. Credit needed to be shared, recognition needed to be given, and backbiting was not acceptable. Caspi describes the atmosphere as one of "incredible trust, camaraderie, mutual assistance, and respect." Gill knew that for the new resource development department to be successful externally, he would need to build a cohesive team internally.

Perhaps the single biggest reason why JDC's culture change eventually took root among JDC's field professionals was self-preservation. Although cultivating donors was a significant amount of work, the money the professionals ultimately received was designated specifically for their program and could not be taken away. In the past, programs funded by unrestricted dollars always ran the risk of being subjected to budget cuts. By bringing in designated funding, Gill and his team brought stability to JDC programs and won over the field professionals who ran them.

Building Systems

JDC is, out of necessity, a highly decentralized organization. For example, a flood in Bulgaria affecting Jews requires immediate, local relief efforts. Bureaucratic involvement from a central office would only hamper relief efforts. At JDC, for the most part, decision-making authority and budgetary control are in the hands of field professionals. This approach has enabled JDC to sustain a highly responsive and entrepreneurial culture when quick action is needed or emergencies arise.

Fundraising, in direct contrast, requires centralized administration. If field professionals in all of JDC's countries worked independently to solicit donors, the results would be chaotic. Federations and individual donors would receive multiple solicitations for multiple projects. These competing efforts would invariably diminish fundraising success and create a highly negative impression of JDC.

Once JDC started a fundraising operation, JDC employees found the centralized nature of fundraising to be contrary to the decentralized way they had operated in the past. Gill imposed a new type of discipline on JDC staff that required all fundraising efforts to go through his department. Although Gill was based in Israel and his initial fundraising efforts focused on JDC-Israel only, his department eventually took over the New York-based fundraising operation as well. This consolidation was the only way that information could be centralized in one place.

The fundraising process requires a sophisticated behind-the-scenes infrastructure to work smoothly and sustain positive donor relations. In order to prepare proposals for donors, program information from field professionals needs to be provided promptly. It is important for fundraisers to have up-to-date accounting data regarding money pledged and money received. Fundraisers need easy access to donor histories, and gifts need to be promptly acknowledged and tax receipts provided. For JDC accounting purposes, designated money needs to be properly credited to the appropriate program when checks come in so that programs in the field can meet their obligations.

Given the far-flung nature of JDC's operations, the only way to accomplish all these fundraising tasks effectively was to use web-based Internet technology, which would allow JDC access to needed information from anywhere in the world.

Gill attempted to create a fundraising system using various people in-house, but the efforts floundered because the individuals working on the system were accountants, not fundraisers, and they lacked the insights into fundraising necessary to upgrade antiquated systems for the new era. After a long period of frustration, Rebecca Caspi volunteered to help build a system that would serve the needs of Gill's team.

In the fall of 2000, JDC hired Gene Philips as its chief financial officer in New York. He had previously worked as the CFO for the Palm Beach federation. Phillips, working closely with Rebecca Caspi and a team of professionals, adapted a widely-used software package, Raiser's Edge, to meet the needs of JDC's resource development department. Through a collaborative effort with the accounting team, the new system effectively flattened and sped up a number of critically important processes.

The system notified appropriate JDC staff immediately when a donation was received so that staffers could call donors, thank them personally, and send an acknowledgment letter in a timely manner. The system also properly credited donations to programs so that the funds became immediately available to professionals in the field. Proposals and documents related to a project were uploaded to the system so that they could become readily accessible for donors if requested. Donor information was entered into a database that enabled JDC to generate reports according to a variety of parameters of interest – nature of the donor, geography, type of program, relationships to other donors, federation affiliation, and so on.

The new system made a considerable difference in JDC's fundraising activities and eliminated much of the confusion and delays that caused problems when the department first began to operate.

Maintaining Program Priorities

When JDC's revenues came primarily from the United Jewish Appeal, JDC had total control over the design of its programs and set its own priorities regarding the programs it chose to fund. Once JDC brought in funding partners, however, it had to adjust. Not all partners were as sophisticated as the Cleveland federation, which had brought in an academic expert to analyze JDC's program proposal for Ethiopian preschoolers. Partners did, however, want to be directly involved and were no longer content simply to write a check.

JDC faced a new set of challenges. While JDC would never allow itself to become donor-driven, implementing low-priority programs simply because donors wanted them, JDC also recognized the new reality – that it would need to become more donor-sensitive. Priorities might need to be modified in order to become more responsive to donors. It was a balancing act. Since JDC only solicits large gifts, its donors tend to be highly successful individuals who want hands-on involvement and expect to see results quickly. The types of social programs that JDC runs, however, cannot be conducted like business enterprises. They do not lend themselves to rapid results. JDC board president Irv Smokler observes, "Business people... don't always feel comfortable with social services projects. We see this over and over again because they don't understand them....most business people don't know how to think like NGO people."[87]

In particular, pilot programs need to be phased in gradually, especially when multiple sites are planned. Success requires ongoing evaluation and monitoring of various implementation factors that can be entirely outside of JDC's control. JDC operates in a dynamic environment that in certain countries is subject to wildly fluctuating events such as war, security and terror crises, population migrations, refugee situations, regime change, graft and corruption, new legislation, banking uncertainties, or economic upheavals. Donors who are accustomed to a more stable and predictable United States environment may fail to fully appreciate just how unpredictable these forces are can be.

In addition, JDC has to constantly make adjustments between realities in the field and donor wishes. Oftentimes, programs are tailored so that donors are satisfied, while simultaneously, the integrity of program priorities is maintained. Donors regularly improve JDC programs by sharing observations and applying their expertise. As one example, a donor couple, while touring the JDC-built Balint Jewish Community Center in Budapest, Hungary, remarked that it needed a fitness center to attract young Jews. Not only did JDC embrace the idea, but the couple eventually donated $200,000 to build one.

Some have observed that despite JDC's philosophy of not wanting to be donor-driven, programs not on JDC's priority list have been implemented solely because important donors wanted them.

JDC keeps careful track of the preferences of particular donors through its donor database. When high-priority

---

[87] Irv Smokler, interview, March 8, 2007.

programs need funding, JDC is able to identify and approach specific donors who have previously shown an inclination to support programs of this type.

Non-Sectarian Programs

One of JDC's biggest dilemmas is how to become more visible to American Jews while honoring its relationship with the federation system. Non-sectarian work is the one area where JDC can engage in fundraising without competing with federations.

JDC began its non-sectarian work during World War I, almost from the agency's founding. At the time, by helping non-Jews in the name of American Jewry, JDC was able to dampen European anti-Semitism, an approach that ultimately helped local Jews. JDC has continued this work throughout its history. Non-sectarian work was done quietly by JDC until the Rwanda genocide in 1994. At the time, Gideon Taylor was responsible for this area within JDC, and he felt that it was vitally important:

> *The non-sectarian programs speak to a segment of our Jewish world that tends to have limited affiliation with – let's call it the system. They are not part of – they are not interested in the system. By the system I mean the organized system, the federations and so on....I think in some ways the system has missed out on that segment of the population. And I felt JDC had a unique opportunity to try to bring some of those people closer to the system in a broader sense....I think the disaster relief was a particularly important way to focus public attention on the Jewish world's commitment to the wider world.*[88]

---

[88] Gideon Taylor, interview, July 31, 2007. Taylor subsequently left JDC and became executive vice-president of the Conference on Jewish Material Claims Against Germany, Inc. He rejoined JDC in 2009.

In a move that was unprecedented at the time, Taylor arranged for JDC to place a full-page advertisement for $60,000 in the New York Times to solicit aid for Rwandan refugees. He brought together a coalition of twenty or so Jewish organizations, many of which had never previously worked with JDC, to co-sponsor the ad.

The result was astonishing – over $2 million in checks arrived at JDC's offices in New York. Some were as large as $10,000 and came from individuals with whom JDC had never previously had contact. Another positive by-product of the ad was that a number of the coalition organizations became knowledgeable about JDC and have since maintained an association with the agency.

Currently, what is now known as the International Development Program (IDP) provides services in almost 30 countries. It sponsors soup kitchens in Argentina for children whose families are living below the poverty line, provides support services for women with breast cancer in Bosnia and Herzegovina, runs HIV clinics in Kazakhstan, distributes wheelchairs and other medical assistive devices in Morocco, and provides help to the hearing-impaired in Turkey. JDC has also responded to natural disasters in a number of countries. The organization provided aid to India, Thailand, Sri Lanka, and Indonesia after the 2004 tsunami, assisted Bangladesh following the country's 2007 cyclone, and helped victims in Kashmir and Peru following local earthquakes in 2005 and 2007, respectively.

In late 2002, JDC initiated a task force to look into its IDP work. The task force felt strongly that IDP was a valuable part of JDC and that this work should be expanded. The decision was then made to make IDP part of all of JDC's external communications.

Claire Schultz, former assistant executive vice-president of global marketing and communications at JDC, describes how JDC's primary focus on international Jewry intersects with IDP work:

The notion of 'tikkun olam,' repairing the world, is a principle that we believe in....[IDP involves] leveraging best practices that have been implemented with the Jewish community to bring assistance and support to the non-Jewish community. It's the same model of operation. I think it's really important, because it's a part of who JDC is, and it says that we're not just focused on [Jews], that we are looking beyond.[89]

At the present time, Will Recant, assistant executive vice-president of JDC, directs IDP. He describes JDC's philosophy regarding the programs it chooses to support:

We have very strategic guidelines behind what we do and how we choose [countries and programs]...We want to work in a community where we can empower a local Jewish community. If a non-sectarian program will help a local community we will look to do something. We will look to work in a moderate Muslim republic – Turkey, Morocco, Tunisia – to help the local Jewish communities that are there and build relationships. We look to bring in Israeli and Jewish expertise into the programs....We work with the U.S. government and look at areas where the U.S. Agency for International Development has a priority interest. That is how we choose the programs that we are involved in.[90]

IDP programs are not on an equal par with programs for international Jewry, and Jewish programs always take funding priority. JDC's budget for these programs is $500,000 annually, primarily to cover staff salaries in New York. However, the efforts of this staff has enabled JDC to leverage another $10 million in designated funding, primarily

---

[89]   Claire Schultz, interview, April 12, 2007.

[90]   Will Recant, interview, August 14, 2006.

through JDC's website, mailbox campaigns, and foundation grants. None of the money used to support IDP programs is annual campaign money from federations. Non-sectarian programming is likely to increase in the future as JDC seeks to reach a new generation.

PART 3: RAISING MONEY

Chapter 7: Funding from Federations

UJC Core Funding and Direct Grants from Individual Federations

In 1993, around the time that Alan Gill joined JDC and federation executives began to scrutinize the national funding system, JDC's total annual budget was $80 million. About 90 percent of this figure was unrestricted, with the federation system providing $55.7 million from overseas allocations by federations to the United Jewish Appeal (JDC's share of the 75/25 split with the Jewish Agency for Israel). The remaining revenues came from unsolicited donations, grants from private foundations, government grants, and Holocaust restitution.

Fourteen years later, in 2007, even though JDC's budget had increased almost five-fold to $353 million, core allocations to JDC from the federation system decreased by one-fifth to $44.6 million. In contrast with 1993, when 90 percent of the budget was unrestricted, only 20 percent was unrestricted in 2007. Of this 20 percent, 13 percent was core funding from the United Jewish Communities, and 7 percent came from JDC's board and a draw on JDC's endowment.

Since unrestricted funding is JDC's "oxygen," needed for basic operating expenses and to leverage various other sources of funding, decreases in unrestricted funding seriously constrain JDC's flexibility.

Designated funding comes to JDC from a variety of sources. In 2007, primarily through the elective funding mechanism created by the ONAD process, JDC generated $34 million in designated grants from individual federations. In total, 2007 JDC revenues from the federation system amounted to $78.6 million.

The $78.6 million that JDC received from federations in 2007 represents slightly less than one-quarter (22 percent) of its total budget that year. JDC, under executive vice-president and chief executive officer Steve Schwager, has been pursuing a deliberate policy of diversifying its revenue sources. The eventual goal is for each type of revenue source to represent 15 percent or less of JDC's total budget. At present, federation revenues are the only exception, giving the federations a highly important role.

The money JDC obtains from federation-designated grants is highly leveraged. Once a partnership is formed with a federation for a specific project, JDC secures additional support for the project from public and private foundations, individual donors, and municipalities and governments in cash and through gifts in kind. This allows JDC to launch and support many programs that would not otherwise be feasible. Designated grants from federations are thus responsible for new program initiatives all over the globe.

Managing Relationships with Local Federations

JDC has, for the most part, continued to honor its 1996 agreement with the federation system not to solicit local donors in a community without first consulting local federation executives. Over the years, the policy has become more nuanced, with different approaches in different communities. Lapses by JDC development staff are relatively infrequent and, in general, federation executives trust JDC. The perspective of Marc Terrill, president of The Associated: The Jewish Community Federation of Baltimore, is typical:

> *There is a high degree of trust....I knew that they weren't going to come in to do anything that was going to damage our own fundraising before the*

annual campaign...that they were going to respect certain rules and boundaries in the community.[91]

Michael Novick, JDC's executive director for strategic development, and Jennifer Kraft, director of community relations, are the two primary individuals with responsibility for relationships with federations. Each has a portfolio of twenty to thirty federations, with responsibility for managing relationships with federation executives, staff, board, and donors. Several other JDC staff also have responsibility for a few federations. Israel-based support staff referred to as account managers are available to produce reports, proposals, and other written documents requested by Novick or Kraft for federations on very short notice. They also help facilitate site visits and missions.

During the era of the United Jewish Appeal, JDC had virtually no relationships with federations. Now, JDC's relationships with individual federations have evolved considerably and are highly complex and individualized. Jacob Solomon, the federation executive in Miami, observes the unique nature of each JDC/federation relationship: "Every time I talk to a federation I get a different picture, and it's just completely fascinating to understand how the intricacy of the community dynamics shape the philosophy of giving to these international agencies."

A variety of factors shape the contours of each JDC/federation relationship and the funding that JDC receives from a particular federation. These include the size of the federation's annual campaign and whether it is growing or static; the federation's historical split between local and overseas allocations; the federation's philosophy on giving to overseas organizations other than JDC and JAFI; the degree of influence that respective JDC and JAFI board members have at the federation; the personal propensities of individual donors associated with the federation; and whether the

---

[91] Marc Terrill, interview, July 27, 2007.

federation is compliant or non-compliant with respect to UJC recommendations regarding overseas allocations.

The amount of the federation's annual campaign and the campaign's yearly growth are perhaps the most significant influences, since the larger the federation and the greater the growth of the annual campaign, the greater the potential revenue to JDC. Thus, the top 19 federations produce 70 percent of JDC's total revenue from federations. Several of the larger federations, like New York and Boston, give directly to JDC.

Since overseas allocations by federations are discretionary, the size of a federation does not necessarily determine how much it gives. Smaller federations can still give significant amounts. For example, the Minneapolis Jewish Federation is approaching almost $3 million a year in giving to JDC, a sizable percentage of its total allocations and the largest per capita allocation to JDC of any federation in the country.

The relationship between JDC and Minneapolis provides a good illustration of how JDC works with federations and the factors that come into play in determining allocations. Minneapolis began to fund JDC programs directly as an outgrowth of the "Who is a Jew" issue in Israel and concern with UJA funding. Minneapolis, along with Cleveland, was one of the first federations to give money outside of the UJA system in the late 1990s and gave much of it to JDC. The relationship between the two organizations has continued to be strong over the years. Dov Ben-Shimon, assistant executive vice-president for board financial resource development at JDC, describes the relationship with Minneapolis as "one of the best examples of the kind of a relationship I would love [for JDC] to have in every federation."[92]

Joshua Fogelson, chief executive officer for the Minneapolis Jewish Federation, describes some of the reasons why his federation has been so supportive of JDC:

> *The areas of focus that JDC identifies resonate with our community's funding priorities....We have*

---

[92] Dov Ben-Shimon, interview, March 14, 2007.

the impression that the programs are well-run, efficiently managed, and extremely well-evaluated, and that's critical to us....Add to that the quality of the presentations that we consistently receive...add to that the continual efforts of the JDC to bring to our community resources that allow us to inform both our donors and also our campaign workers...add to all of that the fact that we have in our community three board members of the JDC, all of whom are passionate about the work that they do; two of whom are past presidents of the federation.[93]

Fogelson's description is largely generalizable to other federations. Federations support JDC's work because they appreciate the professionalism of its programs and field staff, they value its efforts to provide tailored program evaluations, and they benefit from the ways in which it continually educates and informs federation donors and development staff about its programs. JDC does not simply rely on staff to build relationships with federations – JDC's board members are critical in influencing federations to support JDC's work.

The Role of JDC Board Members at Federations

In the 1990s, when overseas allocations by federations were declining and needs in the former Soviet Union were increasing, JDC was much more dependent upon the federation system and looked for ways to address its budget squeeze. One strategy it adopted was to recruit board members associated with particular federations to influence the decisions made by these federations regarding overseas allocations. JDC executive vice-president and chief executive officer Steve Schwager describes the approach at the time:

We looked first to find new people who could be on our board, people who federations were afraid of

---

[93] Joshua Fogelson, interview, July 2, 2007.

but who were involved in federations. And so over a period of years the board changed radically from being an old boy's club or an old girl's club to being much more selective, [consisting of] people who had significant wealth and who wielded power in their communities. And those people were co-opted to advocate for us in their communities.

Later, once the ONAD allocation process allowed federations to engage in elective funding, JDC refined the approach. Nancy Grand, who joined the JDC board in 1995 and had been active at the Detroit and San Francisco federations, pioneered a new initiative that designated a highly engaged JDC board member who was associated with a specific federation as a "champion" for JDC at his or her federation. Grand describes the start of this new role for specific board members:

We had the champions come together and we would give them talking points and information about what to take back to their community for more effective fundraising within their community. And people were quite excited about it….The first morning we had 40 board members come….We got a great speaker and it was like revving up the troops. It was like a pep rally...rather than just at the board meeting telling them, 'go back to your communities,' we would tell them what to say when they went back.[94]

JDC champions, in close partnership with a specific JDC development officer, work to increase designated grants from federations. Alan Gill describes their role:

Our board members are our eyes and ears, and we activate our board members not just as advocates, but as listeners. We want our board members to come back to us and tell us what they are hearing about the

---

[94] Nancy Grand, interview, March 5, 2007.

federation vis-à-vis what's right and what's wrong about the JDC relationship, and we want them to go back to the federation and try to help the federation to see things through our lens as well as advocate for funding.[95]

JDC champions are especially important since JDC staff cannot adequately cover all of the forty or so federations with which JDC has partnerships. About a dozen federations that have the greatest promise for growth are designated as having high priority status and receive a great deal of attention. A second group of 8 or 10 receive special attention as well but are viewed as having somewhat less growth potential. Dov Ben-Shimon describes how JDC champions augment the role of the JDC staff:

We need to empower our...champions because they're the ones that represent us in the community and, just in terms of leverage, give us economies of scale. We can't do that with staff people. We can't do all that work in our federations that we're partnering with. We have forty-something active partnerships with federations – for example, Los Angeles with the Baltics, Atlanta with Minsk, and fourteen federations involved with PACT. All of these things require huge amounts of work, cultivation work. None of it is formal work...you really need that local person who can bridge between the community and JDC and also open the doors to us.

To be a JDC champion, board members need to be passionate about JDC's work and familiar with the details of its programs. JDC champions arrange visits to the federation by JDC field and professional staff, arrange JDC events at the federation, participate in overseas allocations committee meetings at the federation, tell the JDC story to federation

---

[95]   Alan Gill, interview, May 17, 2006.

professionals, identify prospective donors, and ensure that federation missions include JDC site visits.

The role that JDC champions play in identifying prospective donors is particularly significant. Dick Spiegel, a former corporate chief executive officer who chairs the Federation Relations Committee, consisting of all of the various JDC champions, describes an example:

> *It takes time and efforts to get gifts because they don't just happen...you have to cultivate them. And you have to find out what people are interested in, or if they're not interested....Jennifer Kraft...got in touch with a particular individual...who was really not a giver to the [local] federation, but with the permission of the federation, she cultivated him and just recently received a gift of $100,000....Lay people can play a role in that we can help identify those people around the country through our champion group...it's a networking process.[96]*

JDC board members, even those not designated as champions, are usually highly involved with their local federation. Jeffrey Klein, chief executive officer of the Jewish Federation of Palm Beach County, describes how JDC board members operate within his federation:

> *Several of my past presidents have been extremely involved [with JDC]. A past president, while he was a sitting president here, became the president of the Joint. It was the logical progression for him....A lot of my top leadership has been on the board, or has been invited on the board of the JDC. It's been a very symbiotic relationship.[97]*

In contrast with the example of Palm Beach, JDC's visibility

[96] Dick Spiegel, interview, March 5, 2007.

[97] Jeffrey Klein, interview, July 23, 2007.

and influence at a particular federation is weakened when it does not have strong board members there. John Fishel, president of the Jewish Federation Council of Greater Los Angeles, describes what the situation was like for JDC before it had strong board members at the Los Angeles federation:

> *[JDC] had a very low profile here in LA. Lower than in other major communities, and by that I mean that they never had up until maybe the last five to seven years any critical mass of board members from Los Angeles...[The board members] weren't necessarily very active, and they weren't particularly influential in the life of the organization, and the result was that the Joint was not well understood, had no visibility, and had no real advocates here in town.*[98]

Even when JDC has a strong champion at a federation, JDC's degree of influence on overseas allocations can be counterbalanced by the presence of an equally influential member of the Board of Governors of the Jewish Agency for Israel, since the two agencies are continuously competing for elective funding. Each federation has an individual profile with respect to JDC and JAFI board representation. For example, there are no influential board members associated with JAFI at the Minneapolis federation. The JDC voice is dominant there. Allocations to JDC from Minneapolis are consequently high. Palm Beach, another federation with a strong JDC board presence, splits elective funding 50/50 between JDC and JAFI.

When a federation does have a strong JAFI board presence, JDC is less likely to increase its share of the elective funding. For example, the Chicago federation has several prominent members of the Jewish Agency board; in Chicago, elective funding maintains the traditional 75/25 split. Federations such as Detroit, Baltimore, Cleveland, and New York have strong board members from both overseas agencies.

JDC has always encouraged its board members to maintain

---

[98] John Fishel, interview, July 18, 2007.

giving to their local federations, recognizing that their ability to influence the federation is dependent upon their local stature as donors. JDC board members are influential at federations only as long as they are viewed favorably by the federation. Paul Kane, senior vice-president for Financial Resources Development at UJA-Federation of New York, relates the perspective there:

> *We strongly encourage federation donors who are also board members at other Jewish agencies to give us an annual gift that is equivalent to what they give the particular agency. For example, if such a donor were to give the Joint an annual gift of $50,000, we feel that they should give $50,000 annually to UJA-Federation. Over the years, we have been working and coordinating with JDC on this issue, and we have found them to be respectful of our position and responsive.*[99]

How JDC Helps Federations

A federation's annual campaign is the basis for its subsequent allocations. When donors with the capacity to contribute to the annual campaign choose to contribute relatively small amounts or donate elsewhere, it erodes the sense of collective responsibility in the community and adversely affects the federation's revenues. Howard Rieger, former federation executive for Pittsburgh and former president and chief executive officer of the United Jewish Communities, reflects on this trend:

> *Focus [needs to be] on the annual campaign; that is core of support. Without it we're out of business.... [We also need to] think about ways to grow beyond the core, because the annual campaign has got a price point in everybody's mind. Some people have tremendous growth potential, but others have reached*

---

[99] Paul Kane, telephone communication, October 29, 2008.

*what they consider to be the limit of what they're
prepared to give, and yet they've got a lot more money
to give, and they'll buy another product; they're just
not buying any more of the annual campaign.*[100]

All federations have current or potential donors who are
unwilling to give unrestricted money or are unwilling to give
sizable amounts. What JDC offers federations is a way to inspire
these donors to eventually become annual campaign givers by
first getting them involved in meaningful overseas projects.
Rieger describes how he used this strategy in Pittsburgh when
he was the executive:

*Shopping around for places that I could find projects
that would be of interest to our donors, led me to
the Joint...and it's resulted in tremendous support
for the Joint, tremendous support and identity with
the federation on the part of [one] donor...somebody
who essentially was on the sidelines of the federation
became just galvanized by this effort, stepped right
into the middle of the action. And that was a model
that we built upon...people who were pretty much
on the fringe of federation activity stepping up to be
some of our largest contributors on an ongoing basis
through these kinds of ventures.*

Will Recant describes how JDC helped UJA-Federation of
New York inspire donors following a mission to Cuba:

*There is a group from the New York federation that...
gave a token amount, $5,000 to $10,000... but had
potential for six, seven-figure gifts....The New York
professional calls me in and says, 'We have a real
problem with this group. They have tremendous
potential, but they are really not interested in the
federation...they are just turned off to the federation...*

---

[100] Howard Rieger, interview, August 1, 2007.

your job is to give them a Jewish soul.' So I took them for four days to Cuba, and the reality is they walked away with an incredible Jewish soul. They had it before this, but it was brought out during this mission. They said incredible things about what they saw about the community, about the Joint, about the work of the Joint, about their impressions.... The group agreed, with my mediation, that everyone would double their annual gift to the Federation.

One of the most common types of communication initiated by federations to JDC starts with the phrase: "I have a donor who..." Federations are always looking for ways to get donors involved, and frequently consult with JDC to come up with creative ways to reach potential donors. JDC is highly attuned to these needs and works closely with federations to help them cultivate donors. Michael Hoffman, vice-president of Community Planning and Allocations at the Baltimore federation describes his experiences working with JDC:

JDC just has an inherent way of looking at it from the federation's perspective in terms of how we like to steward our donors, how we like to cultivate relationships...it is exceptional customer service... they understand what I need. The donor is a customer....They are able to relate to the customers in a very responsive proactive way that is highly effective.[101]

JDC also offers many opportunities for donors to participate actively in meaningful overseas programs by going on missions. These encounters can be enormously moving. Barbara Bratter, director of planning and allocations at the Jewish Federation of Greater Houston, describes how donors experience federation missions: "[JDC projects] pull at your heartstrings. You are

---

[101] Michael Hoffman, interview, July 27, 2007.

talking about feeding people, feeding elderly. You are talking about providing medicine...because the programs are so — I'll use the word heart-wrenching...people identify with them."[102]

Will Recant, one of JDC's most popular speakers, brings the JDC message to federations since not everyone can go on missions. He describes his approach:

> *There are so many stories that resonate in so many ways because we affect people in the most dramatic way imaginable. So it is a very compelling case. And I make the case to them that local needs have superseded overseas needs....I go through the history of JDC very quickly...and show how the balance has swung to local needs and people aren't thinking overseas anymore. [I explain] what the problems are in Israel, and the needs that aren't being addressed, and how this is a model American organization with accountability and transparency, and we bring this to communities. They love it. So I find that just getting to the basic elements sells very nicely and easily.*

Some donors have particular inclinations toward certain countries, perhaps because their ancestors come from the country or because they are touched by the plight of Jews there. Oftentimes, entire federations will become involved with JDC programs in a particular country because of one donor's passion. JDC works diligently to help connect these donors to projects.[103]

Another way that JDC serves federations' needs is through their staffing strategy. In addition to Novick and Kraft, who serve federations directly, JDC hires additional staff whose specific responsibility is to serve as a liaison between federations and projects in the field. Federation professionals

---

[102] Barbara Bratter, interview, June 26, 2007.

[103] See Chapter 9 for a detailed description of how one donor was inspired to become involved with JDC projects in Belarus.

work directly with English-speaking JDC staff, rather than with JDC field professionals who may not be fluent in English. Jeffrey Klein, federation executive from Palm Beach, describes the advantages of JDC's staffing approach:

> *Rather than the field people being the link to the federations or the individual donors, as the case might be, [JDC] hired young, articulate, talented relationship managers who would be the connection between the project and the person or the federation... and that has been a satisfactory relationship as it relates to federations and donors, to have somebody who [speaks fluent] English...and can...interpret what the federation wants, and what's going on in the field.*

Overall, federations find JDC to be highly responsive, as summarized by Joshua Fogelson of the Minneapolis federation: "[JDC is] extremely focused on service to the federation community...they are extremely solicitous of federations. They make a real effort, and I think that pays dividends."

On occasion, JDC's responsiveness to federations and their donors has a downside. Federations can become unreliable partners when they chase dollars or are too solicitous of donors' wishes. While most federations commit to programs for the long-term, some have funded a JDC program for a few years, only to pull out their funding when donor interests shift elsewhere.

Competition for Elective Funding Between JDC and JAFI

When ONAD created the categories of core and elective funding, it set up a competition for overseas dollars in each federation, primarily between JDC and JAFI, but also with other agencies now eligible for elective funding. In the post-ONAD period, while JDC and JAFI compete for funding, they also share a common desire to see more federation dollars sent overseas. However, neither has been able to significantly influence overseas allocations by UJC.

Over the course of time, JDC has increased its share of the available elective money from 25 percent to at least 50 percent. The remaining share goes either to JAFI or other overseas nonprofit organizations at the discretion of each federation. Once JDC began its efforts to increase its market share of the elective funding, it implemented a blanket policy of firing any JDC employee who spoke disparagingly of JAFI in public. While JDC wished to increase its market share, it wanted to do so through superior customer service, not political attacks.

Alan Gill describes how JDC's operating strategy was not to compete head-to-head with the Jewish Agency but to build relationships with federations:

> We weren't up against the Jewish Agency, but because there were only two agencies involved, it ended up as a zero-sum game. We just basically had positioned ourselves with the federations and had gained their trust and confidence, as well as having educated them about our priority programs, so that when they came down to vote they said, 'We're going to shift money.' And that happened over and over and over again in almost every major federation. There wasn't one federation where we walked away getting less than 25 percent, our baseline number going into this new process, when they started to designate. [In] some we were held constant because JAFI had a strong presence, and we didn't have a strong enough one. And in all the others we gained considerable 'market share'…more important than market share was the sense that we do good work, that we're good partners, that we tell the truth, that when we make mistakes, we tell them.

JDC has been successful at increasing its market share primarily through two avenues, by strategically recruiting board members who exert a strong degree of influence over key federations and by continually refining its customer relations approach. In addition, the governance structure of the Jewish Agency for Israel limits what it is able to do with respect to board recruitment, a situation that favors JDC.

JAFI, unlike JDC, is a quasi-governmental agency based in Israel with a parliamentary-type board representing world Jewry, which means that some of its board members are not from North America. Those board members who are from North America are assigned by federations and UJC, not chosen by JAFI. So JAFI, unlike JDC, is not able to selectively recruit board members based on wealth and influence. This governance structure places it at a distinct disadvantage relative to JDC in obtaining money from federations, since it cannot systematically develop its own "champions" within each major federation to make its case as does JDC.

JAFI's limitation is not entirely a liability, since it has ties to donors around the world. JDC's primarily American board makes it more difficult for JDC to raise money outside of the United States.

Setting aside the board differential, JDC has also been effective at increasing its market share among some federations because they find it is more responsive to their needs than JAFI, which still has a tendency toward bureaucracy. JDC has worked hard to develop a customer relations orientation to serve federations, which constantly need information to make informed funding decisions. Israel and overseas committees at federations will be more inclined to give to an organization that expedites their requests and provides the documents they need.

While the Jewish Agency is not as consistent as JDC, it has made progress in developing a customer service orientation, learning from JDC's example. Jeff Kaye acknowledges that "the Jewish Agency started 8-10 years later and is rapidly catching up."[104] He credits Alan Gill's foresight in cultivating relationships with federations, so that when UJA collapsed, JDC was poised

---

[104] Jeff Kaye, email correspondence, September 14, 2008.

to develop new approaches and operate independently. JAFI in contrast, still has an umbilical cord to UJC because of its heavy reliance on federation funding, and it has taken much longer for JAFI to learn how to respond to the changing federation environment.

As one example of how JAFI still needs to improve, an Israel and overseas committee chair at a federation requested information about a Jewish Agency program, only to receive a document in Hebrew. He was not fluent in the language. Even when it was subsequently translated for him, he could not make sense of the budget. Another federation professional describes his experiences with each agency:

> *The only time that the Jewish Agency comes in is to ask us for money. JDC will come…they say how are we doing? What areas do we need to beef up? Here are some things that are going on. No discussion about money. Stewarding the relationship.*[105]

Once federations became empowered to decide where to spend elective funding, some of them began to consider overseas agencies other than JAFI and JDC. At the same time, various overseas agencies began to aggressively court federations. Lee Wunsch describes his experiences in Houston:

> *We are getting calls once or twice a week from NGOs in Israel looking for money. And that is a phenomenon that I don't know how anybody is going to get control of….We try to talk to everybody, but we don't…give them all money. But there are some cases where we have sought out providers, where we have tried to partner with organizations that have some presence in Houston….The brightest example that we have been working on is with Hadassah, [which has a] very strong presence in Houston, they do a*

---

[105] The individual sharing this observation asked that it be used without attribution.

lot of work in Israel, and we have...created this very
successful partnership between Hadassah and the
federation funding some youth programs in Israel
and the hospital.

While the Houston federation selectively supports particular overseas agencies, other federations such as Philadelphia have thrown the door wide open and fund a number of agencies.[106] These types of situations make it harder for JDC to obtain elective funding, since with more players in the game, there is potentially less money for JDC.

Federations consistently rate JAFI's programs on an equal par with JDC's and, despite the intense competition for funding between JDC and JAFI, the two organizations work cooperatively in the field. Todd Stettner of Kansas City offers his observation on the degree of cooperation:

I think the cooperation on the ground...between
JAFI and JDC...has been good. You take out the
competition for funding and those kinds of issues,
and when they actually have to work together, I think
they do a pretty good job.

Trends in the Federation System and Implications for JDC

Although JDC has been highly successful at cultivating partnerships with individual federations to obtain designated gifts, JDC still relies heavily on core allocations from the federation system and must therefore pay close attention to this funding source. Projections of current trends – among donors, individual federations, and the federation system overall – suggest that JDC's core funding will become increasingly imperiled.

Individual donors are unlikely to reverse the historical trend toward increased designated giving and away from

---

[106] The Center for Israel and Overseas at the Jewish Federation of Greater Philadelphia gives $7.8 million annually to a variety of agencies.

unrestricted giving. More designated gifts, both within and outside of the federation framework, appear inevitable, with corresponding implications for annual campaign revenues.

Individual federations are becoming increasingly independent and dissatisfied with UJC, while peer pressure to preserve the collective system among federation executives is waning. In the future, it is likely that there will be less overseas giving by federations, and the money they do send will increasingly go directly to overseas agencies rather than through UJC.[107] It is also likely that JDC and JAFI will have to compete with an increasing number of other agencies for this funding.

Overseas allocations continue to decline for the federation system as a whole. The pool of money that is split between JDC and JAFI will only continue to shrink. There appears to be little likelihood, following UJC's failure to prevail during the ONAD process, that JDC will be able to alter the 75/25 split formula and increase its share of the core. How JDC addresses this decline in core funding remains to be seen. It is almost certain that the JDC board will be called upon to play a major role.

---

[107] In 2008, Los Angeles and Philadelphia made decisions to allocate their overseas money directly to overseas agencies, bypassing UJC altogether.

Chapter 8: The Crucial Role of the JDC Board

New Financial Expectations of Board Members

Up through 1997, the year that board president Jonathan Kolker established the Warburg Society, revenue from the JDC board was minimal.[108] Until then, JDC did not communicate any financial expectations to its board members – it only encouraged them to be generous to their local federation. Through Kolker's efforts, board members gradually began to join the Warburg Society, pledging $250,000 or more to be paid over the course of several years. By the time Kolker's presidency ended in 2000, annual revenues from the board through the Warburg Society had risen to $8.4 million.

When longtime JDC board member Eugene Ribakoff became the new board president of JDC at the end of 2000, he felt that JDC needed to expand board giving beyond the Warburg Society framework. From his experience, JDC had the only board "where members don't have financial obligations," which made it an anomaly in the nonprofit world, since virtually all other nonprofits expected board members to contribute.[109] Ribakoff asked board member Nancy Grand to serve as the resource development chair and work on changing the board's culture.

Ribakoff felt it was time for JDC to institute an unrestricted

---

[108] See Chapter 4 for a description of the origins of the Warburg Society.

[109] Gene Ribakoff, telephone communication, September 25, 2008.

annual board fund. This would communicate the new expectation of giving and bring in additional undesignated revenue that, it was hoped, would offset the decline in core funding from UJC. However, Ribakoff recognized that his idea would not be an easy sell, so he asked Grand to obtain unanimous agreement from her resource development committee before launching a campaign. She encountered a great deal of resistance from the committee but prevailed through sheer force of personality:

> *It got to be a challenge...a huge challenge....The people on my committee came up with every reason not to do it...but I just kept calling them and each time countered their objections....They kept saying, 'Well we have never done it before.' And I said, 'Well yes, that is how you change the culture. You do things that haven't been done before'...so I finally, finally got my consensus....I was allowed to go in front of the executive committee...[and] somehow it passed....[Later, at a meeting of the full board with 150 members], people raised their hands...and said it is wrong and I told them what I thought.*

Board members who were already giving designated money to a specific JDC program were now being asked to give yet again to an undesignated fund. Art Sandler describes a typical reaction: "It upset a lot of board members because there are a lot of us...who give JDC a lot of money, but we don't make an annual board gift."

Even after overcoming objections from the resource development committee, the executive committee, and the full board, Grand faced yet another constraint – Ribakoff asked her not to solicit at board meetings. His rationale was entirely reasonable – he did not want board members to be offended or uncomfortable when they came to board meetings. Yet from Grand's point of view, board meetings were the only time when she could talk with board members face-to-face.

Despite all of these obstacles, the first annual board campaign raised $1.3 million in unrestricted funding.

Current Board Giving

In 2007, JDC's board members gave approximately $20 million to JDC. Of this amount, $3.4 million went to the annual unrestricted board fund, and the remainder consisted of designated gifts.

The Board Giving subcommittee is currently chaired by Jane Weitzman, corporate vice-president of the international shoe company Stuart Weitzman. She describes how she encourages board members to give to JDC's annual board campaign:

> *I let everybody know how I feel about it. I have made several speeches at board meetings. I also organized some of my friends on the board to make phone calls because it was impossible for me to do it all myself. And then Steve [Schwager] has been very helpful as the executive vice-president with backing this. He has made it clear that this is the direction he wants the organization to go in.*[110]

Almost all of the approximately 150 board members now donate to the board campaign.[111] Philanthropist Lynn Schusterman, who has been involved with JDC since 1992, makes the largest annual contribution.

Penny Blumenstein, a Detroit-based philanthropist who chairs the Resource Development Committee, comments about the change in giving to the annual board campaign over time:

> *There was nothing compelling board members to give to JDC unless a particular project happened to appeal to them. They never thought about making*

---

[110] Jane Weitzman, interview, March 6, 2007.

[111] JDC senior staff also donate to the annual board fund.

an annual commitment and didn't appreciate how
reductions in core funding have affected JDC. So I
think we have done an amazing job because almost
everyone is now participating.[112]

Designated giving to JDC by board members has also grown. Board members have varying motivations for giving designated gifts to JDC, which support a broad range of JDC programs. Some board members started out as donors and later were invited to join the board, while others started out as board members and later became donors.[113] Some give in response to a crisis.

The late Henry Everett was a longstanding board member who decided in partnership with his wife Edith Everett that JDC would be the best organization to implement programs to support Israel's Druze communities.[114] There are approximately 120,000 Druze in Israel, a distinct non-Arab, non-Muslim minority group. The Everetts felt strongly that this group deserved more support:

> *My husband and I felt that the Jewish community*
> *here and [in Israel] were not doing the right thing*
> *for [the Druze] population. And it bothered us for*
> *many years, but it didn't seem that anyone was*
> *really all that interested....We used to talk about*
> *what to do and finally...we decided that we would*
> *allocate what was a very large gift for us to try and*
> *do something for that community, to demonstrate to*
> *the community...that there were people who were*
> *concerned about them. The organization that was the*
> *best one we could imagine to do the on-the-ground*
> *work was the JDC. And they were very responsive to*
> *the possibility of this gift and how we would go about*

---

[112] Penny Blumenstein, interview, March 8, 2007.

[113] See Chapter 9 for a detailed description of how one donor's involvement with JDC led to a board nomination.

[114] When Henry Everett died, his wife Edith joined the JDC board.

it. And we always thought very highly of the JDC and their operation. They seemed to be very serious. Our impression is that money is used wisely, and there are a lot of caring persons in that organization.[115]

Board members often become inspired to give after meeting Jews served by JDC. As one example, board member Myra Kraft, a Boston-based philanthropist who is president and director of the New England Patriots Foundation, provides support to JDC to help Kafkazi Jews in Israel. Kafkazi Jews, also known as Jews of the eastern Caucasus or Mountain Jews, are a little-known group who emigrated from Azerbaijan between 1970 and 1990. They have their own language, Juhuri, which is related to Persian. She describes a transformative encounter with a Kafkazi family:

It was hard to understand why [the Kafkazi Jews] were different....After we went to Azerbaijan, we came back to Israel, and we went in Acco to a home where there was a grandfather, his mother, the daughter, and her daughter....the grandmother was dressed in traditional clothing. The grandfather was a very proud looking man, lovely gentleman.... The daughter said, 'In Baku my grandfather was an elder in the community and people came and spoke to him and wanted his advice. Here no one comes. No one speaks to him.' And it was really poignant. I got it. And I think everyone sitting in that room got it, really understood the huge cultural difference. It wasn't like coming from Moscow or St. Petersburg. It was coming from an area that had its own beautiful culture and traditions and way of life, living in the mountains, surrounded by Muslims and having to live a certain way, protecting their language, having

---

[115] Edith Everett, interview, March 8, 2007.

therefore a very hard time learning Hebrew or refusing to learn Hebrew.[116]

It is not uncommon for board members to give spontaneously, inspired in the moment by a crisis. Will Recant describes one such incident:

> *Jane Weitzman was the chairperson of our Latin America Committee when the crisis in Argentina happened on December 31, 2001. By January 1 we were already talking to UJC about raising extra money for the needs in Argentina. I turned to Jane and said, 'You know that thousands of Jews have fallen below the poverty line. We are afraid this coming Passover – which is a couple of months away – that people aren't going to be able to make their own seders. We are thinking that it might be nice if to have a communal seder. Generally, around the world, we go in the other direction. We teach Jews how to make seders for themselves at home, but in Argentina this year people can't afford it. We want to pay for everybody who can't pay.' She asked how much we needed. We said, '$125,000.' Jane and her husband Stuart gave us a check immediately.*

JDC's professionalism, transparency, and rigorous program evaluation are factors often cited by board members as reasons for giving. Board member S. Lee Kohrman describes why he is comfortable giving to JDC through his federation and the foundation he directs:

> *Their accounting is transparent....I saw how they spend every dime, and I saw who was working on it. I saw who the caliber of people were. I knew exactly what they were getting and how the money was being spent, who was getting what. And I always*

---

[116] Myra Kraft, interview, February 21, 2007.

*added up my bank account, and the bank account
came together. And I knew ... we were getting a bang
for the buck and that we had lots of evaluation and
assessment by the Myers-JDC-Brookdale Institute.*

Improving Board Engagement

Board giving was only one aspect of the board in need of
change. In December 2004, Judge Ellen Heller succeeded
Eugene Ribakoff as JDC board president. She had retired
from her role as Judge of the Circuit Court for Baltimore the
previous year. To prepare herself for the presidency, shortly
after her nomination, she began calling board members to find
out how they felt about JDC and their board involvement. She
ended up speaking with close to half of the 150 or so board
members before assuming office.

Consistently, these conversations identified the engagement
of lay leadership as an area for improvement. During Ribakoff's
board presidency, a board engagement task force was convened.
The task force determined that JDC needed a staff member
dedicated solely to the board, so a new staff role was created
at JDC, director of board relations. Based on her conversations
with board members, Judge Heller concluded that while this
new position was a positive development, more needed to be
done:

> *[I wanted] to try and engage our lay board members
> in a stronger partnership with the professional staff....
> there were comments about an imperial presidency or
> not hearing from the presidents or all of the decision
> making being made between the president and the top
> professional. Here's this wonderful organization that
> everyone loved and our attendance has always been
> so high at the board meetings, but really not feeling
> that you had great input into what was happening...
> so I decided that for a healthy organization and
> for other reasons as well, in an era where we are*

soliciting donor support and soliciting funds, you've got to have an engaged board.

Her desire to create a more inclusive atmosphere was viewed by everyone as "a breath of fresh air," in the words of one board member. Throughout JDC's history, going back to Felix Warburg, JDC had been run by a small group. While board members were always consulted, decisions were ultimately made in a top-down fashion by the board president and executive vice-president. It was clear to Judge Heller that perpetuating this style no longer served JDC's interests. It also would no longer work since board members were now donating money to the organization and wanted more input into decision-making. If JDC wanted its board members to contribute, it needed to give them more of a voice.

Judge Heller, with the support of executive vice-president and chief executive officer Steve Schwager, convened a Lay Leadership Engagement Committee that was commissioned to make recommendations that would improve lay engagement, examining such critical areas as governance, financial and administrative oversight, policy setting, fundraising, and communications. The committee's report, the result of careful consensus, laid out a series of recommendations in considerable detail. One of them involved the creation of a new subcommittee called Donor Base Expansion that would focus on finding new donors and engaging the next generation of Jewish philanthropists.

Donor Base Expansion

Eighty percent of JDC's board consists of individuals in their 60s and older who have achieved considerable wealth. A viable future for JDC requires that it attract new donors and board members with the same level of resources and commitment to the organization.

JDC has not been particularly successful at engaging younger donors. Individuals in their 30s and 40s who have financial resources may not yet be philanthropically oriented. Those who are inclined to give are unlikely to be content just writing a check – they want direct, hands-on involvement with programs. JDC cannot readily offer this involvement since its programs are overseas.

Jodi Schwartz, a partner in a Manhattan law firm who is one of JDC's younger board members, provides a perspective on the inherent difficulties that arise when attempting to attract younger board members:

> *There's enormous wisdom, experience, and wealth in older Jews. But we also need to be relevant to younger people...the Jewish world is huge and hard to break into...to be told in 30 years you can have a place on the board because the youngest person [on the board] is 60 in the real world, that's not acceptable. So we definitely have to figure out a way to keep the strengths of the predecessor generation, and their wisdom, and their experience and their commitment, and their reflexive love of Israel...and at the same time, become relevant and interesting... because the truth is that if we wait until [potential board members] are finished having their families and get involved with 30 other organizations...we're going to lose them.*[117]

When the Lay Leadership Engagement Committee recommended the creation of the Donor Base Expansion Committee, it was partly with an eye toward younger donors. Accordingly, the chair was given to Jacob Schimmel, the youngest member of the JDC board. Schimmel, who is in his 40s, is the London-based chairman of UKI Investments, which has business interests in Western and Eastern Europe, the United States, Africa, India, and Israel.

Schimmel recognized that his first priority, even before attracting younger donors, was to reorient the board's

---

[117] Jodi Schwartz, interview, April 11, 2007.

thinking about fundraising. Everyone on the board needed to become cognizant of the organization's requirements for increased funding. Through board members' participation on area committees, they had been learning about JDC's programs and budgetary requirements but were not necessarily engaged in resource development on behalf of the organization. He describes his perspective regarding the committee he chairs:

> *It's quite clear that a board member's responsibility is not just to sit there and make some decisions in relation to how monies are spent, but they also have a responsibility for the future sustainability of the organization...therefore, every one of the board members, not just my committee, but every one of the board members needs to understand and appreciate that their responsibility as a board member is to resource develop....We are trying to integrate this resource development discussion in every single subcommittee at every single level so that everybody takes responsibility.[118]*

When it was first formed, Schimmel's committee started out slowly. Only when the committee expanded to 25 members did things begin to happen. Over the course of time, Schimmel integrated members from the various area committees onto his committee, so that each area committee had two representatives. The idea was to have ongoing discussions about funding needs between those who were concerned about programs around the world and those who were responsible for finding resources to fund the programs. The integration of resource development with area committees would ensure that funding sources would always be part of these conversations, which had not necessarily been the case previously.

Schimmel himself has taken an active role in interesting his business associates in JDC's work, pioneering a new model

---

[118] Jacob Schimmel, interview, March 8, 2007.

that combines business with philanthropy. Rather than asking business associates unfamiliar with JDC to donate directly to the organization, he instead asks them to consider receiving a smaller return on their investment in a given business venture, with the balance going to the local community for programs administered by JDC. He always invites these business associates on trips to communities served by JDC so they can see programs first-hand. He describes what often happens when they visit: "Once I get them there, the sale is just simple... [one business associate who] never knew anything about JDC's work ...came with me... saw the work of the JDC [and] said, this is absolutely incredible."

Irv Smokler, who became JDC's board president in 2008, sees Schimmel's approach as the wave of the future:

> *Jacob Schimmel is one of the few people in my opinion who is way out ahead of the curve....He's thinking of ways of combining business with philanthropy.... [He] may be one of the few people who...is so smart and so gifted in that area and so dedicated that if you could build a business model for JDC as another way of raising money, Jacob could do it...Business people want to be connected in ways that they feel comfortable with, which is business.*

Beyond interesting business associates in JDC, Schimmel recognizes that trips to JDC sites are essential to become an effective board member:

> *Professionals within the organization have to engage their leaders fully so that they're educated, so that they understand what's happening. In order for that to happen, we have to go out and see the programs and become inspired and impassioned to make the case because it doesn't work otherwise....That's an extremely critical part, to engage, educate yourself and become passionate about your organization so that you*

*can go out and make sure that your organization has
the funds that it needs...you cannot support [JDC's]
work without knowing what's happening...in order to
do that, you have to do missions.*

Dov Ben-Shimon, who works closely with the board in his staff role, agrees that getting board members more deeply involved is essential for fundraising, since engaged board members are more inspired to give and to talk about JDC to their friends:

*The more engaged [board members] are, the better
donors they are, the more they want to contribute, the
more they're infusing us, and it translates also into
the financial future of JDC because an engaged board
member [creates]...this snowball effect of bringing
in his or her friends, donating more, recruiting more
friends to come. We're finding more and more that
board giving is becoming a referral system as well.*

Board Relations

The JDC board is deeply committed to JDC because they identify with its mission and because they respect the organization's effectiveness at carrying out its mission. Board member Andrew Tisch, co-chairman of the Board and chairman of the Executive Committee of Loews Corporation, reflects on the JDC board's degree of commitment:

*The level of commitment in the board members
is astounding...I think one of the great strengths
of the organization is that the mission is so clear
and so well presented that the board adopts it very
quickly....There is great simpatico between what the
professionals see as their mission and what the board
sees as its mission, and that's why I think the board
is as effective as it is. That may be one of the unique*

things about JDC in all of Jewish philanthropy and
all of philanthropy in general...there is a tremendous
understanding of the mission, a tremendous buy-in to
the mission.[119]

The board identifies so strongly with JDC's mission not just because of what JDC does, but also because it has staff members who are responsible for cultivating, educating, and training board members. Nadine Habousha, the director of board relations, the position created when Eugene Ribakoff was board president, oversees a multifaceted function that includes orienting new members and finding mentors for them, identifying strengths of board members to spotlight leadership potential, planning board meetings, and showcasing JDC's work so that board members understand JDC's programs in the field.

To inform board members about the field, Habousha oversees a team of regional specialists who are assigned to various area committees and serve as links between the field and the board. The regional specialists convey information to board members and JDC. Through their contacts with JDC field staff, they provide board members with accurate, up-to-date information about programs around the world. And, through their contacts with the board, they provide JDC with information about specific board members. The information that regional specialists provide enables JDC to identify board members who are engaged, involved, and making contributions to the board's work.

Board members' terms are renewed every four years based on a review of their activities conducted by the Nominating Committee. Alan Gill is one of two JDC staff members assigned to the committee. Former board president Eugene Ribakoff describes what JDC looks for in a board member:

> *We don't want board members just to be on our*
> *board and to have their name there. We want them*
> *to be active, to visit our programs, to serve on area*
> *committees, to attend meetings. We have a requirement*

---

[119] Andrew Tisch, interview, February 15, 2007.

for attending. If you don't attend meetings, we ask you to leave the board.

Contributions by board members can be either financial or non-financial. However, if financial contributions are made without other, non-financial contributions, they are deemed insufficient. A board member who contributes financially but is otherwise uninvolved, failing to attend meetings, go on missions, or talk about JDC is not the type of board member JDC desires. In contrast, members whose financial contributions may be relatively modest but who are highly engaged, grasp the issues, contribute to the work of their committees, go on missions, and advocate for JDC are appreciated and valued. The ideal is to have board members who, in the words of board member Jodi Schwartz, contribute "work, wealth, and wisdom."

Keeping board members engaged and interested is an ongoing challenge. Board members are highly accomplished and want to be involved in a fashion that allows them to contribute their expertise. However, the size of the board, JDC's international reach, and the complexity of JDC's work sometimes makes it difficult for newcomers to get involved in a meaningful way. Whenever a new board member joins, one of JDC's concerns is whether the individual will find a way to contribute and put his or her talents to use.

Unlike many nonprofit boards, JDC's board members are interested in the details. Presentations to the board are not "broad brush" pictures but carefully articulated descriptions of work in the field describing both successes and problems. Because discussions can become quite sophisticated, JDC carefully selects individuals to give these presentations, leaning toward professional staff who are skilled at leading discussions that draw upon board members' varying types of expertise. Presenters try to be as honest as possible about challenges in the field, not only because board members appreciate the candor, but also because they are often able to provide a fresh perspective and offer helpful advice based on their own backgrounds.

JDC and the Board – Dilemmas and Challenges

The past decade has seen significant changes in the way that JDC relates to its board. For 80 years, there were no financial expectations of board members. Now, virtually 100 percent of the board contributes to JDC's core undesignated funding through the annual campaign. Board members make significant designated gifts and are more highly engaged, working more closely with JDC professionals. These changes all have ramifications that will affect the role of the board in JDC's future.

The Elite Nature of the Board From a board that was once dominated by major federation donors, the JDC board has now expanded to include individuals who are not strongly connected to federations. While there are a few academics and Jewish leaders who contribute important expertise to JDC, the vast majority are Jews in the upper echelons of wealth. As JDC's board becomes increasingly dominated by this elite group, there is a risk that it will lose some of its ability to represent the concerns and interests of the larger Jewish population, including the rising generation of Jewish leaders.

Limits on Board Giving As JDC's core funding from UJC continues to decline, JDC is almost certain to turn to its board for replacement funding. This is simply because those who have already donated to the organization and have a passion for the mission of the organization are far more likely to give than individuals who have never donated to JDC. The risk that JDC faces is that its board will "max out" if too much is asked of them.

Increasing Board Influence The more the board gives, and the more engaged the board is, the more the board will end up influencing JDC's policies, programs, and strategies. JDC has always been run by a highly competent coterie of professionals who have a sophisticated understanding of social programs. Regardless of the degree of achievement, competence, and intelligence possessed by board members, their expertise, usually attained in the business arena, is not a match for JDC professionals in the field.

JDC has already begun to face situations in which prominent board members offer money for specific programs that have not been identified as JDC priorities. In these circumstances, should JDC become donor-driven and shift valuable field personnel to such projects, or should it remain need-driven and run the risk of alienating the board member? The middle ground that JDC has established in these types of situations is to be what JDC calls "donor-interactive," recognizing that money given to fund a lower priority program may very well lead to money later for a higher priority program. In the long-run, JDC's ever-present funding needs and the board's increasing role in helping to meet these needs can only create tensions that JDC will need to resolve.

Globalizing the Board   While the JDC board does have members from Canada, the UK, Australia, and Israel, it is dominated by Americans. This geographic concentration corresponds to JDC's donor concentration. JDC raises about $5 million annually from donors outside of the United States, which is a small amount relative to the funds it raises from American sources. Even though there are wealthy donors in the UK, Canada, and Australia who give to international Jewish causes, their money goes to JAFI and Israel. JDC has not been able to shift the ideological orientation of these donors, which means that the financial burden for supporting Diaspora Jews round the world falls on Americans. JDC recognizes that it needs to internationalize its board in order to strengthen fundraising outside of the United States.

Chapter 9: Becoming a JDC Donor

JDC in Belarus

The country of Belarus, which declared independence from the Soviet Union in 1991, is bordered by Lithuania, Poland, the Ukraine, and Russia. Ruled by President Alexander Lukashenko since 1994, Belarus is generally considered to be Eastern Europe's last remaining dictatorship and has been described by former Secretary of State Condoleeza Rice as an "outpost of tyranny," a classification shared with Cuba, Iran, and North Korea.[120] Dissent is not tolerated and its citizens are subject to numerous restrictions on religion, freedom of speech, the press, and freedom of assembly.[121] Among Eastern European countries, the U.S. Agency for International Development ranks the operating environment for non-governmental organizations such as JDC in Belarus as one of the most difficult.[122] NGOs are closely monitored by the authorities.

Originally known as Belorussia, Belarus and surrounding

---

[120] Opening Statement by Dr. Condoleezza Rice, Senate Foreign Relations Committee, January 18, 2005. Retrieved from http://foreign.senate.gov/testimony/2005/RiceTestimony050118.pdf.

[121] Central Intelligence Agency, The World Factbook. Retrieved from https: www.cia.gov/library/publications/the-world-factbook/geos/bo.html.

[122] 2007 NGO Sustainability Index for Central and Eastern Europe and Eurasia, The U.S. Agency for International Development. Retrieved from http://www.usaid.gov/locations/europe_eurasia/dem_gov/ngoindex/.

areas were part of the Pale of Settlement, a portion of the Russian Empire where Jews were allowed to live under the tsar. At the end of the 19th century, Belarus had a Jewish population of 725,000 and was an important and thriving center of Jewish life and culture. Its major cities were more than 50 percent Jewish. In the early part of the 20th century, before the Russian Revolution of 1917, many of its Jews emigrated to the United States.

More than 90 percent of the Jews who did not choose to emigrate were murdered under Stalin and Hitler. Many of those who survived did not return to the country. Currently, Belarus has an estimated Jewish population of about 50,000, with about half residing in Minsk, the capital.

JDC operates a number of programs for Jews in Belarus that are similar to those offered in Russia and other republics of the former Soviet Union. JDC serves about 17,000 elderly Jews in the country, providing food, medical support and equipment, home care, and day centers where the elderly can socialize. The organization also provides food and other aid to families with children at risk. In addition, JDC offers a variety of Jewish renewal programs to reconnect Jews with their heritage, which include cooking classes, Hebrew lessons, literary groups, and cultural programs.

Program expenses of approximately $5 million annually are covered by JDC's budget for countries comprising the former Soviet Union. The Jewish Federation of Greater Atlanta helps support a community center in Minsk called the Minsk Jewish Campus through a partnership with JDC.

Learning About JDC

Barry M. Ginsburg and Merle Z. Gross-Ginsburg were accomplished business professionals when they met in mid-life and married, each for the second time. Barry had served as the chief operating officer and director of Dansk Designs, and later became vice-chairman of the Chelsea Property Group, which operates Chelsea Premium Outlets around the United States. Merle was the first woman partner in a major commercial real estate firm in New York City, Edward S. Gordon and Company, now part of CBRE, and among her many achievements was the renovation of the Chrysler Building. She founded and served as the first president of the Association of Real Estate Women in Manhattan, a networking organization for women in commercial real estate.

Neither Barry nor Merle grew up in families that had financial resources. Although the Ginsburgs were involved with a number of charitable organizations over the years, they gave primarily of their time and expertise, rather than money, since until they retired, their assets were tied up in illiquid real estate. When they did begin giving, their preference was to give to causes where they could see results and have direct relationships with the recipients of their giving. Merle describes their philosophy: "When we give money we like to see a direct impact. We are not big on supporting infrastructure of large organizations...we prefer giving directly to the agencies that we are involved with."[123]

Although there was some giving to Jewish organizations, Jewish causes were not a particularly high priority for them. Their donations to federations were considerably below their capacity.

Barry's maternal grandparents were among the emigrants from Belarus who came to the United States in the early years of the 20th century. Growing up, Barry was very close to his grandparents, but he did not develop a personal interest in Belarus until several years after his retirement in 1999, when he attended a family wedding. At the wedding, he reconnected with a long-lost cousin who was raised as a Christian but wanted to learn about the Jewish side of her family. Inspired by the reunion, he surprised everyone at the wedding by announcing that he would take the whole family to "Russia" to explore their roots.

Barry subsequently hired a genealogist to learn about his ancestors and discovered that they came from Belarus,

---

[123] Barry and Merle Ginsburg, joint interview, July 6, 2007.

not Russia. It was a country he had never heard of. He made thirty copies of the genealogy report and distributed them to his family, creating a considerable buzz. Upon researching arrangements for the family trip, however, he was advised that the political situation was precarious and that he should wait. It was not safe for a busload of American Jews to be traveling through the Belarusian countryside.

Soon thereafter, Barry and Merle received a totally unexpected letter from Jerry Spitzer, a JDC board member, inviting them to accompany an upcoming JDC board mission that was going to Hungary, Poland, Rumania, and Bulgaria. Spitzer was a good friend of the parents of one of Barry and Merle's daughters-in-law, and it was from them that he had learned about the Ginsburgs' interest in Eastern Europe. The Ginsburgs knew nothing about JDC but were intrigued. Although they were not particularly interested in JDC or its work, they did see the mission as an opportunity to visit Europe and Belarus. They asked if JDC could help them arrange a trip to Belarus after the mission.

Before leaving, they discreetly sat in on an area committee meeting at a JDC board meeting in New York City, where they were introduced to JDC's country director for Belarus. The Ginsburgs agreed between themselves that they would make a donation of $10,000 to JDC as a goodwill gesture.

JDC routinely assigns development officers to accompany missions. Abe Wasserberger, a senior development officer at JDC, was selected to accompany this mission, which consisted of 10 couples. Upon receiving the list of participants, he immediately spotted the Ginsburgs and wondered who they were. No one at JDC seemed to know. He finally learned that they had been invited by the Spitzers.

Wasserberger's role on missions is to cultivate and strengthen relationships with donors. His approach requires considerable finesse, and he starts by making everyone on the mission comfortable. He takes photos to engage participants and tries to find common ground for conversation.

At the start of the mission, Wasserberger found that the

Ginsburgs "had their antennae up"[124] because they were unfamiliar with JDC and did not want to be solicited for money. Barry, who tends to be very direct, asked Wasserberger during their very first conversation what he did for JDC. Wasserberger explained that he was a fundraiser and told Barry about his social work background.

As the mission traveled through Eastern Europe, Wasserberger checked in with each of the couples on the mission several times a day, including the Ginsburgs, offering to help in whatever fashion he could. He learned from the Ginsburgs that they were planning a trip to Belarus after the mission, which he had not known about.

Wasserberger immediately contacted Stuart Saffer, the country director for Belarus at the time, to share his impressions, and the two began to strategize an itinerary for the upcoming visit, emphasizing Barry's interest in his origins. In the meantime, the conversations between Wasserberger and the Ginsburgs became increasingly friendly and open as the couple shared their personal stories with him.

Over the course of the mission, the Ginsburgs visited a series of homes inhabited by JDC aid recipients. Merle describes what she saw:

> *When you see the homes in the shtetls, you feel that you are being brought back one or two hundred years. They are exactly the same now as they were then. You feel like you could be in a Tolstoy or Dostoyevsky novel.*[125]

They also toured JDC restitution properties, where their respective real estate backgrounds allowed them to contribute

---

[124] Abe Wasserberger, interview, July 10, 2007.

[125] Merle Ginsburg presentation, Belarus and Moldova Area Committee, American Jewish Joint Distribution Committee Board Meeting, October 17, 2006.

meaningfully to discussions and engage intellectually.[126] Despite their newcomer status, they were treated no differently than anyone else on the mission. Both were "incredibly impressed"[127] by the JDC programs they saw.

What was equally impressive to them was the commitment of the board members on the mission. Several of these board members had "adopted" specific countries and had been supporting JDC programs in these countries since JDC entered Eastern Europe following the fall of communism. In addition to personal donations, they had also been raising money for these programs through their federations. These board members had continued to support these programs for a decade or longer and had been returning on a regular basis to monitor their progress. It was clear to the Ginsburgs was that there was a warm, ongoing relationship among donors, program officials, and aid recipients and that these programs were transforming Jewish lives.

Inspired by the example of others on the mission and engaged both emotionally and intellectually in JDC's work, Barry asked Wasserberger if Belarus had a major donor. Wasserberger recalls his response to Barry. He wanted to convey to the Ginsburgs that they had the potential to change several generations of Jewish lives in the country:

> *Outside of the Joint as an organization, I don't think there has been a significant donor in the past generation. You are it, Barry, you, and a few others who are now emerging in this group that's developing under your leadership. You can change the Jewish community of Belarus. You can make a lasting impact throughout the country. And he just said 'Wow,' he said it on an exhale.*

---

[126] Following the fall of communism, Jewish communal properties such as synagogues, schools, hospitals, and cemeteries that were seized by the Nazis and communist regimes began to be returned to Jewish communities in Central and Eastern Europe and the former Soviet Union. JDC has been heavily involved in this restitution process through the World Jewish Restitution Organization.

[127] Merle Ginsburg presentation.

Barry and Merle continued to ask questions of Wasserberger about the costs of various programs throughout the rest of the mission, which indicated to him that they were beginning to think about what they might eventually contribute. A bond began to develop between the Ginsburgs and Wasserberger. Wasserberger communicated regularly with Saffer throughout this process and speculated that the Ginsburgs might be willing to give as much as a six-figure gift, even though Wasserberger had not asked them for a donation or discussed a specific amount.

Barry subsequently asked Wasserberger whether his inclination was to ask for a specific dollar figure. Wasserberger responded:

> *It is my particular style of fundraising never to focus the relationship on a dollar amount, but to put the issue out there that needs to be resolved. Only after donors have a full understanding of what the problems are and what the potential solution is, at that point, at the bottom line on the balance sheet of the budget, they themselves will discover the number. But I never tell them what the number is. It's a part of a discovery process that they have to feel themselves. Otherwise, I'm just a salesman, rather than someone interested in building a relationship. Our aid recipients do not have the option of shopping around for another NGO – as Jews, they know that if it were not for JDC, they would have no one else to turn to. Our work requires that we make a long-term commitment to them. So when we present needs to donors, we tell them here's what it costs to save a life or maintain a life. To be true to ourselves, we at JDC have to be more relevant to life and less focused on numbers.*

When the board mission ended, Wasserberger said goodbye to the Ginsburgs. They agreed to reconnect upon their return to the United States. The Ginsburgs proceeded on to Minsk.

Donor tours are exhausting. For any JDC country director, taking donors on a tour of JDC program sites is one of the most intensive parts of his job. Every stop must be carefully scheduled, planned, and orchestrated in advance. During the trip, the group travels continuously from morning to night, and the country director must be "on" constantly, attentive to every nuance, and totally focused on what is happening. He or she must read the donors constantly but unobtrusively, watching for signs of interest or boredom, energy or fatigue, and has to be attentive to the dialogue between spouses to ascertain what interests them and how they make decisions about whether to donate. Small details like rest stops become extremely important. There is no time off.

Stuart Saffer prepared an extensive four-day itinerary based on information that both the Ginsburgs and Wasserberger provided regarding their specific interests and inclinations. Saffer was hopeful that they would eventually support some of JDC's programs in Belarus.

The Ginsburgs' first full day in Belarus happened to coincide with Victory Day, May 9th, during which Belarusians celebrate the defeat of Nazi forces by the Soviets in Berlin. In Minsk, on Victory Day, Jews from all over Belarus gather at the Yama memorial, which commemorates the World War II massacre of 5,000 Jews from the Minsk ghetto whose bodies were thrown into a massive pit. Erected in 1946, the memorial was the first in a Soviet country to specifically commemorate the murder of Jews. The Ginsburgs witnessed a military parade and a solemn ceremony at the memorial, which they found highly affecting.

That afternoon they went to what JDC calls a "warm home" in the small village of Lepel, near Vitebsk, where once a month, the 10 or 15 Jews who still live in the village gather for food and a Jewish program. Saffer describes how the Ginsburgs reacted:

It was their first interaction with Soviet Jews, and they're looking at most of these people in their 70s and 80s. And the first thing that comes across to any donor is thank God my grandparents had the common sense to get up and leave because if it wasn't for their decision 100 years ago, I would be sitting here waiting for JDC to give me the package. That's a real humility lesson...if it wasn't for my grandparents making that decision, I'd be the one sitting at the table here every month.[128]

A Jewish veteran wearing his war ribbons talked about his experiences during World War II. It was such an emotional encounter that both Barry and Merle were moved to tears. The Ginsburgs made a note to themselves that the refrigerator in the home was not working. They then traveled to Vitebsk and spent the evening at a local hotel.

The next day, Saffer arranged for a local Jewish historian named Arkady Shulman to join them as a tour guide. They toured Vitebsk, where artist Marc Chagall was raised, and then stopped at the Vitebsk Jewish community center, where Barry and Merle sang and danced with local Jews. In talking with them afterward, Barry and Merle met several who were familiar with the local villages where Barry's ancestors had been born. They noted that the community center was unfinished and made a few inquiries, drawing on their real estate background. The remainder of the day was spent in the village of Ula, not far from Vitebsk, where Barry's maternal grandparents were born. They were able to visit several sites that were linked to his ancestors. They then traveled to Minsk.

On the road from Vitebsk to Minsk, Saffer recalls a conversation with Merle:

She was telling me how they've been involved in many causes in their life, and many charities, and many different organizations, and given their time,

---

[128] Stuart Saffer, interview, July 12, 2007.

and Merle had said one of my friends told me recently that if we don't give to the Jews, then no one else will. And Merle looked at me, and she said it with absolutely certainty, that this was the real truth for her at this stage in her life. She said, 'It's up to me and Barry now to make our impact with the Jewish community, and the Jewish world in our own small way, because if we don't do it, no one else is going to do it.'

In Minsk, the Ginsburgs went on a tour of the Minsk Jewish Campus and were asked to represent American Jewry in a ceremony involving the donation by JDC of medical equipment to the local prosthetic limb manufacturing plant. They then visited the village of Sklov. Saffer had arranged for a Jewish press correspondent to be present and made sure the Ginsburgs were profiled on the Minsk Jewish Campus website so they could see the story upon their return home. He also organized a meeting with a local real estate developer who gave them an interesting tour of a local high-rise construction site. Saffer comments on these arrangements:

> *[There is] a lot of micromanaging of all of these very, very small details, which in my mind are crucial for making sure you build a solid relationship with a donor....When I approach working with a donor, I believe that you have to show both the high-level needs and the low-level needs in terms of funding.... It's also crucial showing the small details, showing how we at JDC are sensitive to the small things.... There's also a need to connect donors, if possible, by their professional area.*

At the end of the trip, Barry and Merle asked if they could spend some time alone with Stuart, and the three sat down at a restaurant. In a simple and straightforward fashion, they proceeded to describe how they wanted to contribute. Over the course of the trip, they had been taking notes, and compiled a list of JDC programs they wished to support:

- new refrigerator for the warm home in Lepel
- completion of the Jewish community building in Vitebsk
- food, medical, and other services for children and families at risk in the Vitebsk region
- meals for the elderly in Vitebsk
- two university scholarships for Jewish students
- discretionary fund for the use of the country director

When the visit came to an end, Saffer returned to Israel, and the Ginsburgs returned to the United States.

Giving to JDC

Around the time that the Ginsburgs returned to the United States, Wasserberger contacted Saffer, who briefed him extensively about the trip and his impressions. He then called Jerry Spitzer and asked him to contact the Ginsburgs and learn how they felt about JDC and the visit to Belarus. Once Wasserberger had the complete picture, he called the Ginsburgs and invited them to JDC's offices in New York. He wanted them to meet Steve Schwager. Wasserberger describes his logic:

> *I felt...they were at a point on the fence where they were either going to make a minimal gift and feel good about it, or were going to take a risk based on another leap of faith and trust and make a major gift. And that's where I thought Steve could play a vital role in that they would now meet the top guy in the organization. And that was important to their psyche, that they have a private meeting with the head of JDC. Barry's been the top guy...why do they*

want to fool around with the middle man? I'm the middle man. Steve is a very impressive leader and meetings like this can solidify intangibles such as trust, integrity, and confidence.

After lunch with Schwager, Wasserberger met with the Ginsburgs alone and they discussed a preliminary proposal. No numbers were mentioned, just programs and the period of time that the programs would be funded. Then, working with Saffer and other JDC staff, Wasserberger generated a formal proposal. The resulting document was fairly complicated, but Wasserberger felt the Ginsburgs would want to see all of the details. He sent it to them and subsequently met with them again for over 90 minutes, reviewing each element carefully.

At the end of the meeting they agreed to it, "just like that" in Wasserberger's words. The amount they would be giving was $202,000, more than twenty times the figure they had originally decided to donate before the mission and visit to Belarus. Barry explains why:

Working with the Joint in a small country, where seemingly nobody else is interested other than the Joint itself...for a really relatively modest amount of money, hundreds of thousands of dollars, you can make an incredible difference, and you can see it and taste it, and you can see people appreciate it. It is a remarkable thing. And I don't know really where else for that kind of money you would have the same impact. I don't think anywhere and that really struck us.

Even while the Ginsburgs were agreeing to support the programs described in the JDC proposal, they were thinking about other ways to help Jews in Belarus. Although they had visited the country in May, they were made aware of how cold it was there during the winter. Most of the homes did not have central heating, but instead received heat from poorly-insulated pipes emanating from a central heating plant. They could see that this inefficient system could only result in considerable heat loss. Saffer had asked in passing if they knew of any sources of warm clothing.

Barry and Merle asked their friends in the clothing business, but no one they spoke with was willing to donate. So they decided to make a donation themselves. They started by asking a friend who supplies clothing to Wal-Mart to produce a prototype of Barry's favorite fleece sweatshirt at a factory in China. When the first prototype came back with material that was too thin for winter, they asked for another, which turned out to be satisfactory.

It was at this point that they emailed Saffer to let him know about their new idea and asked him if it would be useful for people in Belarus. They ultimately ordered about 5,000 sweatshirts in two colors, in sizes from toddler to XXXL, enough to fill a 20 foot shipping container. They even had a little logo added, consisting of a G for Ginsburg superimposed over a samovar, one of the few items Barry remembers his grandparents brought over from Belarus. The total cost was about $40,000, including manufacturing and shipping.

The Ginsburgs subsequently went on a second visit to Belarus to investigate another new program idea, an interest-free microloan program for Jews who wanted to start their own businesses. The Ginsburgs had suggested the program to Saffer, and he responded with enthusiasm.

While they were interested in pursuing the idea, a number of concerns needed to be addressed. First, they wanted to be sure that there was interest. Saffer arranged for them to meet with around thirty individuals who had expressed entrepreneurial aspirations. One wanted to start a restaurant. Another envisioned starting a computer consulting business. A third wanted to start a printing company. Barry noted that virtually all of the people they met with were men, so he made sure that women would also be eligible and encouraged to participate.

The Ginsburgs were also concerned about the banking

system in Belarus, since the banks were owned by the government. Saffer directed them to the one privately-owned bank in Belarus, which had been started by a car dealer in Vitebsk in order to improve business by providing loans to car buyers. Barry and Merle met with one of the bankers, who had an MBA, and they were reassured that the financial dealings of the microloan program would be properly administered.

Another concern was small business training – could citizens of a former communist dictatorship with no business experience run a successful enterprise? Saffer, at the suggestion of the Ginsburgs, helped develop and initiate a new training program to be administered by JDC that would initially enroll twenty aspiring business owners and meet over the course of ten weekends.

There was one more concern raised by Barry and Merle that could not be resolved on this visit – to what extent would the government interfere? President Lukashenko was an advocate of communism, not capitalism. His government had a track record of declaring half-ownership in businesses that became successful. Starting a business involved obtaining 61 permits from 11 different agencies. The Ginsburgs spoke with someone in Minsk at the local United Nations small business development office about these concerns but could not get a straight answer. They would need to proceed cautiously.

Once the pieces were in place, the Ginsburgs committed additional resources for the microloan program along with two other donors from Atlanta and Los Angeles. They came up with the acronym CHELP, for Community Helping Entrepreneurs Loan Program. They had now pledged nearly $500,000 for JDC programs, even though they started out knowing nothing about JDC.

Following the two trips, Saffer made sure that the Ginsburgs received photos and descriptions of the programs they were supporting. He even arranged for the refrigerator in Lepel to be stocked with food, since the Ginsburgs had not thought of that detail.

In October 2006, Saffer arranged for the Ginsburgs to be

guest speakers at the Belarus and Moldova area committee at the JDC board meeting in New York. Some of their children and spouses attended with them. Participants witnessed a moving slideshow with photos of the couple's first trip to Belarus and descriptions of their positive experiences with JDC.

Merle was subsequently nominated to the JDC board and was officially welcomed in December 2007. She joined in large part to help JDC become more visible among her peers:

> *I have certainly been in the Jewish world for the last twenty years. I had never heard of the Joint…for the work that the Joint does, for us not to know about it – I think there is something lacking…since I think it is such an extraordinary organization…it needs to get its message out in a substantial and meaningful way.*

Merle was inducted into the Warburg Society in May 2008. In June 2008, the Ginsburgs brought 36 members of Barry's family, ranging in age from 8 to 77, to Belarus on the long-awaited trip to explore their roots. Barry and Merle had now come full circle from that first public declaration at the family wedding several years earlier.

AFTERWORD

Jonathan D. Sarna
Joseph H. & Belle R. Braun Professor
of American Jewish History
Brandeis University

The American Jewish Joint Distribution Committee (JDC), its historian Yehuda Bauer recounts, "has always prided itself on being a philanthropic organization run on business lines."[129] The organization's German-Jewish founders, businessmen and bankers for the most part, considered themselves stewards of the communal funds they received. They maintained meticulous records and strove to keep their books in balance.

Bauer articulates four central principles that have guided JDC since its founding in World War I:

- *A pledge of impartiality* – it steers clear of political involvements and takes pride in being "probably the only really nonpartisan organization in Jewish life."
- *A commitment to help Jews help themselves* – notwithstanding its frequent focus on relief and rescue, its overriding aim is to "to help Jews rebuild their lives as self-respecting, upright, independent human beings, who would neither rely on humiliating doles nor have to seek them."
- *A belief that Jews must be helped wherever they are* –

---

[129] Bauer, 1974, p. 19.

"that Jews have a right to live in countries of their
birth, or in a country of their adoption."

- *An obligation to supervise and administer funds
  carefully and efficiently*

These principles form the background for the story so ably
recounted here by Mark Rosen.

Rosen stresses three central themes – money, conflict,
and institutional change – that, while rarely considered in
standard institutional histories, are absolutely critical to
understanding JDC, and, as it turns out, many other aspects
of Jewish organizational life as well. In opening these themes
to scholarly analysis, he makes a major contribution.

The first theme, *money*, is, of course, the lifeblood of any
organization. Despite JDC's efforts to operate on business
principles, its income for many years proved highly volatile.
In 1915, amidst reports of World War I atrocities, it brought
in over $6.1 million (almost $130 million in 2008 dollars). Ten
years later, as American Jews turned inward and expected JDC
to wind down its work, the organization's receipts shrank to a
mere $206,195 (just over $2.5 million in today's dollars). In the
depths of the Great Depression, when Polish Jewry faced acute
starvation, JDC managed to raise only $385,225 ($6,017,631
today), so small a fraction of what was needed that one of its
leaders suggested that the organization close down entirely.

The creation of the United Jewish Appeal (UJA), in 1939,
as the central fundraising instrument for Jewish relief and
rehabilitation in Europe, immigration and settlement in
Palestine, and aid to refugees in the United States relieved
JDC of fundraising responsibilities. The idea, in an era of
centralized planning and government coordination, was for
Jewish fundraising to be similarly centralized and streamlined.
JDC, according to this plan, could focus on its original goal: the
distribution of funds. The funds themselves would be collected
by the UJA.

As Rosen explains, however, this proved easier said than
done. The formula that determined what percentage of UJA

money would go to JDC, what percentage to the United Israel Appeal (the Jewish Agency for Israel), and what percentage to refugee care became a perennial source of acrimony and tension. Needs invariably outstripped funds, and communal priorities remained in dispute.

In the final years of the twentieth century, the UJA funding mechanism broke down completely. The opening up of the former Soviet Union imposed new demands on JDC, UJA fundraising proved less successful than before, and efforts to change the distribution formula to increase the amount of money available to JDC foundered. A cool-headed analysis by JDC, informed by the sound business principles to which the organization was committed, made clear that a financial crisis lay just over the horizon. The resulting quest for a reliable stream of money to fund JDC operations and allow it to fulfill its mission set the stage for the new fundraising initiative that Rosen so ably describes.

JDC's quest for funds placed it into direct conflict with other organizations collecting funds for Jews abroad, most notably the United Israel Appeal (UIA), which channeled funds to the Jewish Agency, and several other Zionist organizations. *Conflict*, for this reason, is the second crucial theme of Rosen's discussion, and distinguishes this work from much previous writing about Jewish philanthropy which focuses upon lofty ideals – "collective responsibility!" "to dwell in unity!" "we are one!" – to the exclusion of painful realities.

Conflict, of course, is commonplace in American Jewish communal life reflecting as it does both the competitive ethos of American free market capitalism, and long traditions of Jewish disputation (*mahloket*). But in the case of JDC and UIA, conflict also fed upon deeper ideological and historical roots. The inter-war years had witnessed a fierce controversy between JDC, which raised funds for Jewish agricultural settlements in Russia ("Agro-Joint"), and the Zionists, who believed that money should go to Jewish agricultural settlements in Palestine. JDC argued that "Jews must be helped wherever they are" and viewed its work in Russia as part of its mandate to help Jews help themselves. The Zionists insisted that the best way help Jews help themselves was to return as many of them as possible to their Jewish homeland. By World War II, Agro-Joint was dead, its leaders purged by Stalin in 1937-38, and the thousands of Jews whom the Joint had optimistically settled on the land were now either starving refugees or victims of the Shoah. History thus seemed to have ruled decisively in favor of the Zionists, and in 1941 Abba Hillel Silver, then head of the United Palestine Appeal, did not mince words in assessing blame:

> *These practical philanthropist[s]...proposed highly practical schemes for the settlement of Jews on the land...in Crimea, in Biro-Bidjan, elsewhere, in fact, everywhere except in Palestine. And Jews listened to them and were completely persuaded and their tens of millions of dollars went into these highly practical and philanthropic activities. One doesn't speak any more of Crimea and Biro-Bidjan. They have now joined the limbo of all other lost territorialist adventures. As for Eastern and Central European Jewry, what is there to show for the vast expenditures of monies and energies of two decades but graves and ruins and devastated communities and burned synagogues and myriads of panic-driven refugees.[130]*

JDC's return to Eastern Europe in 1989, following the collapse of communism, rekindled this ideological struggle. Once again, JDC, true to its principles, sought to aid Jews "wherever they are" and the Zionists, now the leaders of the State of Israel and the United Israel Appeal, countered with their own principles, insisting that the only way to make Jews truly safe was to bring as many of them as possible back to their homeland. The controversy that ensued over how to allocate overseas funds – how much to Israel, how much to the

---

[130] A.H..Silver, "The Cause of Zion Must Not be Minimized "as quoted in Stock, 1987, p. 112.

Joint – replayed, in many ways, the earlier controversy. Only this time, the Zionists were determined to win.

For its part, Rosen shows, JDC was reluctant to take up this battle directly. Its leaders and funders had for decades been strong supporters of the State of Israel, and JDC itself carried on highly important work there. A public dispute with Israel over the formula for allocating UJA funds carried myriad risks. Moreover, UJA's fundraising was itself faltering; receipts were down year after year. So while supporters of Israel focused on gaining a larger share of the UJA funds, JDC's leaders recognized that an entirely different solution to the organization's funding problems needed to be found so that it could carry out its work in Eastern Europe independently. Michael Schneider, Jonathan Kolker, and Alan Gill arrived at that different solution, and, in the process, transformed JDC as an organization.

How these and other leaders devised and implemented JDC's new fundraising program is the fascinating story that Rosen recounts in this narrative, and at the deepest level it is a story about *institutional change* – the third of Rosen's grand themes. Coming to JDC as an outsider, Gill sensed long before others did that JDC's funding problems, the UJA's fundraising problems, and the disputes with Israel over allocations were all symptoms of a much deeper structural change taking place within Jewish philanthropic life itself. An older model beholden to the value of "communal responsibility" was breaking down. Wealthy donors were growing reluctant to turn their funds over to communal agencies like UJA for allocation and disbursement based on "communal priorities"; they demanded much greater personal say in how their money was being allocated and spent.

Building on this insight, JDC underwent extensive change. JDC went back into the business of fundraising, establishing an innovative, highly individualized strategy directed to wealthy donors and worked hard to obtain "designated funds" from individual federations, once that became possible. As a result, JDC transformed its budget from one largely reliant on unrestricted UJA funds to one heavily dependent (over 80% in 2007!) on closely restricted donor contributions. In order to support this new fundraising structure, JDC also totally transformed its institutional culture to focus not only on those in need, but also, more than ever before, on "donor relations."

All of this happened, Rosen shows, in a period of less than a decade with less conflict than might have been expected.

By being highly attuned to changes in the Jewish and general philanthropic worlds, and by working in concert with local Jewish federations, JDC reinvented itself and quintupled its annual budget while remaining true to its central mission, upholding the core principles that have guided JDC since its founding. Along with the remaking of Hillel, a story recounted elsewhere by Mark Rosen, this is one of the most successful stories of institutional transformation in the recent history of the American Jewish community.

REFERENCES

Anders, Władysław. 1949. An Army in Exile: The Story of the Second Polish Corps. London: Macmillan.

Bauer, Yehuda. 1981. American Jewry and the Holocaust: The American Jewish Joint Distribution Committee, 1939-1945. Jerusalem: The Institute of Contemporary Jewry, Hebrew University.

--------- 1974. My Brother's Keeper: A History of the American Jewish Joint Distribution Committee, 1929-1939. Philadelphia: Jewish Publication Society of America.

Beth Hatefutsoth (Tel Aviv, Israel), and Edith Zertal. 1984. To Save a World: American Jewish Joint Distribution Committee (AJJDC) 1914-1984. Tel Aviv: Beth Hatefutsoth.

Bubis, Gerald B., and Steven F. Windmueller. 2005. Predictability to Chaos? How Jewish Leaders Reinvented Their National Communal System. Baltimore, MD: Center for Jewish Community Studies.

Dekel-Chen, Jonathan L. 2005. Farming the Red Land: Jewish Agricultural Colonization and Local Soviet Power, 1924-1941. New Haven: Yale University Press.

Ginzberg, Eli. 1942. Report to American Jews on Overseas Relief, Palestine and Refugees in the United States. New York: Harper & Bros.

Handlin, Oscar. 1964. A Continuing Task: The American Jewish Joint Distribution Committee, 1914-1964. New York: Random House.

Henry, Marilyn. 2007. Confronting the Perpetrators: A History of the Claims Conference. London: Vallentine Mitchell.

Hessel, MeLena. 2007a. "The Genesis of the United Jewish

Appeal." Electronic copy, Cohen Center for Modern Jewish Studies, Brandeis University.

--------- 2007b. "JDC and the Soviet Union: Refugees and Re-entry." Electronic copy, Cohen Center for Modern Jewish Studies, Brandeis University.

--------- 2007c. "The Life of ONAD: Its Origins, Operation, and Demise." Electronic copy, Cohen Center for Modern Jewish Studies, Brandeis University.

Hoffman, Charles. 1989. The Smoke Screen: Israel, Philanthropy, and American Jews. Silver Spring, MD: Eshel Books.

Kolker, Jonathan W. 2005. Incompatible Ideologies: The Conflict Between the American Jewish Philanthropists and the Ideological Zionists in the Twentieth Century. Unpublished manuscript.

Leavitt, Moses A. 1953. The JDC Story; Highlights of JDC Activities, 1914-1952. New York: American Jewish Joint Distribution Committee.

Raphael, Marc Lee. 1982. A History of the United Jewish Appeal, 1939-1982. Brown Judaic Studies, no. 34. Chico, CA: Scholars Press.

Sarna, Jonathan D. 2004. American Judaism: A History. New Haven: Yale University Press.

Shachtman, Tom. 2001. I Seek My Brethren Ralph Goldman and "The Joint:" The Work of the American Jewish Joint Distribution Committee. New York: Newmarket Press.

Spector, Stephen. 2004. Operation Solomon: The Daring Rescue of the Ethiopian Jews. Oxford: Oxford University Press.

Stock, Ernest. 1987. Partners and Pursestrings: A History of the United Israel Appeal. Lanham, MD: University Press of America.

Weiner, Anita. 2003. Renewal: Reconnecting Soviet Jewry to the Jewish People: A Decade of American Jewish Joint Distribution Committee (AJJDC) Activities in the Former Soviet Union, 1988-1998. Studies in Judaism. Lanham, MD: University Press of America.

APPENDIX A: TABLES

Table A1: JDC Annual Budget in Retrospect, 1992-2007			
Budget Year	Unrestricted Funds	Total Budget Including Partner Funds	Unrestricted Funds as a Percentage of Total Budget
1992		$65,437,900	
1993		61,156,200	
1994		68,688,300	
1995		70,217,800	
1996		69,982,000	
1997		70,440,900	
1998		66,460,400	
1999	$66,645,500	190,590,606	40.0%
2000	68,987,100	196,239,592	35.2%
2001	66,887,100	192,338,471	34.8%
2002	65,899,200	243,166,562	27.1%
2003	67,587,300	249,158,755	27.1%
2004	69,240,093	257,155,158	26.9%
2005	67,006,529	266,360,404	25.2%
2006	69,220,741	320,410,019	21.6%
2007	69,475,561	352,751,013	19.7%

Note: JDC began recording partner funds in 1999. Before 1999, the JDC annual budget was primarily the unrestricted funds received.

Source: JDC

Budget Year	Unrestricted Funds	Partner Funds	Total FSU Budget	FSU Budget/ Total JDC Budget
			Table A2: JDC Former Soviet Union Budget in Retrospect, 1989-2007	
1989			$620,000	
1990			3,000,000	
1991			2,700,000	
1992			5,375,000	
1993			6,074,600	
1994			9,161,600	
1995			11,557,400	
1996			11,116,100	
1997			11,097,400	
1998			41,331,633	
1999	$18,177,600	$33,378,645	51,556,245	27.1%
2000	20,259,500	41,611,775	61,871,275	31.5%
2001	17,363,700	53,693,690	71,057,390	36.9%
2002	19,235,000	50,503,339	69,738,339	28.7%
2003	18,503,100	54,622,003	73,125,103	29.3%
2004	18,476,996	73,576,392	92,053,388	35.8%
2005	17,960,273	72,852,580	90,812,853	34.1%
2006	17,885,468	82,289,507	100,174,975	31.3%
2007	17,069,237	98,734,141	115,803,378	36.1%

Note: JDC began recording partner funds in the FSU in 1998. Before 1998, the FSU budget was primarily the unrestricted funds.

Source: JDC

Table A3: Overseas Allocations from the Federation System, 1986-2006					
Year	Total Campaign Dollars (in millions)		Campaign Dollars Overseas (in millions)		Percentage Allocated Overseas
	Actual Dollars	Adjusted for Inflation	Actual Dollars	Adjusted for Inflation	
1986	$692	$1,292	$350	$654	50.6%
1987	730	1,316	368	663	50.4%
1988	744	1,288	358	620	48.1%
1989	759	1,254	370	611	48.8%
1990	758	1,188	358	561	47.2%
1991	740	1,113	331	498	44.7%
1992	734	1,072	312	456	42.5%
1993	724	1,027	313	444	43.2%
1994	719	994	298	412	41.5%
1995	719	970	289	390	40.2%
1996	727	952	286	374	39.3%
1997	741	954	274	353	37.0%
1998	765	969	271	343	35.4%
1999	795	981	270	333	33.9%
2000	827	987	273	326	33.0%
2001	851	999	275	323	32.3%
2002	832	954	274	314	33.0%
2003	828	932	262	295	31.6%
2004	856	933	266	290	31.1%
2005	878	925	267	281	30.4%
2006	896	921	270	278	30.1%

Note: Base year for inflation adjustment is 2007.

Source: JDC

APPENDIX B: INDIVIDUALS INTERVIEWED

Note: Individuals are listed below according to their affiliation at the time of their interview.

JDC: Judy Amit, Dov Ben-Shimon, Herbert Block, Yitzhak Brick, Rebecca Caspi, Arieh Doobov, Rina Edelstein, Haim Factor, Zvi Feine, Diana Fiedotin, Alan Gill, Ralph Goldman, Eliot Goldstein, Vivian Green, Jack Habib, Nadine Habousha, Gideon Herscher, Sara Hirschhorn, Yifat Kariv, Jennifer Kraft, Antony Korenstein, Linda Levi, Arnon Mantver, Michael Novick, Asher Ostrin, Gene Philips, Danny Pins, Jonathan Porath, Will Recant, Arik Rosenblum, Galit Sagie, Dana Sapir, Stuart Saffer, Susan Bougess Sawicki, Michael Schneider, Claire Schultz, Steve Schwager, Alberto Senderey, Yossi Tamir, Abe Wasserberger

JDC Board: Penny Blumenstein, Edith Everett, Nancy Grand, Judge Ellen Heller, Alan Jaffe, S. Lee Kohrman, Jonathan Kolker, Myra Kraft, Gene Ribakoff, Art Sandler, Jacob Schimmel, Jodi Schwartz, Irv Smokler, Dick Spiegel, Andrew Tisch, Jane Weitzman

JDC Consultants: Darrell Friedman, Jack Ukeles

JDC Donors: Barry and Merle Ginsburg

Federations: Barbara Bratter (Houston), Hope Cutler (Palm

Beach), John Fishel (Los Angeles), David Fleshler (Cleveland), Joshua Fogelson (Minneapolis), Michael Hoffman (Baltimore), Stephen Hoffman (Cleveland), Suzanne Jacobson (Houston), Paul Kane (NY), Jeffrey Klein (Palm Beach), Steve Nasatir (Chicago), John Ruskay (NY), Jacob Solomon (Miami), Todd Stettner (Kansas City), Marc Terrill (Baltimore), Lee Wunsch (Houston)

United Jewish Communities: Doron Krakow, Howard Rieger

Jewish Agency for Israel: Alan Hoffman, Jeff Kaye

Claims Conference: Gideon Taylor

Other: Saul Andron (previously with JDC), David Sarnat (previously with JAFI)

INDEX

Footnotes are indicated in page numbers as: "page number"+*n*+footnote number" Example: Brinkley, Joel, 19*n*21

World War II, 13–14, 15

Jewish Agency for Israel and, 32

"Jewish continuity" programs and, 35–36

ONAD and, 71

Overseas Connections initiative and, 60

Soviet emigration and, 19

tax laws in United States and, 32n38

United Jewish Communities, in creation of, 67, 69

See also federation system

United Jewish Communities (UJC)

allocating money, 52, 113, 114, 115, 117

core funding, 99–100

creation of, xvi, xvin2, 37, 67–69, 67n67

funding of JDC, xvii

ONAD and, 69, 70–71, 80 (*See also* ONAD)

on ONAD process, 81–82, 81n78

rate of decline in donors and, 76–77

United Palestine Appeal (UPA), xiv–xv, xvn1, 8–10, 10n17, 11, 13, 14–15

United States

entering World War II, 12–13

Jewish organizations, 5

relief agencies, 6, 152

Soviet Jews emigration to, 18, 19n21, 20, 24

tax laws in, 32n38

in World War I, 5

U.S. Agency for International Development, 95, 135, 135n122

U.S. House of Representatives, and Soviet hunger crisis, 27

USDA (U.S. Department of Agriculture), funding to JDC, 27, 28

USSR *See* Soviet Union

V

Victory Day, in Belarus, 142

Vitebsk (Belarus), 142–144, 145, 148

W

Wachsstock, Susan H., 67n67

Wallenberg, Raoul, 13

Warburg, Felix, 5, 6–7, 9, 126

Warburg Society, 53–54, 119, 149

"warm house," 142

Warsaw ghetto, 13

Wasserberger, Abe, 138–139, 139n124, 140–141, 145–146

Weinberg, Harry, 29–30

Weinberg Foundation, Harry and Jeanette (Baltimore), xviii, xviiin3, 29, 44

Weiner, Anita, 24n32

Weitzman, Jane, 120, 121n110, 124

Weitzman, Stuart, 121

Weizmann, Chaim, 8, 14

Wertheimer, Jack, 37n47

West Germany, 29

See also Germany

Windmueller, Steven F., 67n67, 157

World Jewish Restitution Organization, 140n126

World War I, 3, 5–6, 152

World War II, 12–13, 26, 28, 38–39, 142, 154

World Zionist Organization, 9

Wunsch, Lee, 35–36, 36n43, 115–116

Y

Yama memorial (Belarus), 142

Yudelson, Larry, 37n46

About the Author

Mark I. Rosen, Ph.D. teaches in the Hornstein Jewish Professional Leadership Program at Brandeis University and does strategic research and consulting for Jewish organizations. He lives in Newton, Massachusetts.

The Fisher-Bernstein Institute at Brandeis University is dedicated to strengthening the infrastructure of the Jewish community by educating leadership in fundraising and philanthropy. To this end, the Institute generates research, develops instructional materials, and offers programs for those concerned with fund development in the Jewish community. The Institute was established in 1997 by a gift from the late Max M. Fisher, philanthropist and community leader. Its name honors the partnership between Mr. Fisher and the late Irving Bernstein, a partnership that produced extraordinary results in raising funds for the Jewish people.